MAXIMUM
MINI

The essential book of cars based on the original Mini

Jeroen Booij

Veloce Classic Reprint Series

Other great books from Veloce –

Veloce's other imprints:

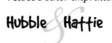

Also available ...
Apps
Download now from
www.digital.veloce.co.uk

Also available ...
eBook
Download now from
www.digital.veloce.co.uk

Hubble & Hattie

Belvedere

www.veloce.co.uk

First published in March 2009 by Veloce Publishing Limited, Veloce House, Parkway Farm Business Park, Middle Farm Way, Poundbury, Dorchester DT1 3AR, England. Fax 01305 250479 / e-mail info@veloce.co.uk / web www.veloce.co.uk or www.velocebooks.com.
Reprinted June 2017. ISBN: 978-1-787111-18-9; UPC: 6-36847-01118-5.

MAXIMUM
MINI

The essential book of cars based on the original Mini

VELOCE PUBLISHING
THE PUBLISHER OF FINE AUTOMOTIVE BOOKS

Veloce *Classic Reprint* Series

Contents

Foreword

Back in the early seventies, if, like me, you didn't like ordinary cars, you just built your own. At least that is what I did. I bought a £60 scrap Mini Van and designed an incredibly strong spaceframe to bolt its 850cc engine and running gear on. The body design was very simple so I was able to make it myself. I riveted on 18 gauge aluminium panels and ended up with a buggy sort of thing that was 300lb lighter than a Mini and bloody good fun. It had 15 per cent more weight on the rear wheels as a result of moving the petrol tank and driver's position rearwards, ultimately creating a car that handled really well; it was named the IGM Minbug (pictured below). Having just married, my wife and I had planned to drive the Minbug around Europe. However, a couple of friends decided they wanted one, too, so instead of the European holiday my wife was there helping, drilling and riveting alongside me! During the time I owned my Minbug I did 40,000 miles in it. It was great fun and practical; I never should have sold it. For over ten years I looked for a surviving example, and had just about given up when a Dutch chap rang saying he thought he'd found one. It turned out to be true, and after all these years I found myself reunited with my Minbug.

The Minbug was not the only Mini derivative Jeroen had tracked down, as you'll see in this book, which is packed with vehicles, some of them truly innovative and surprising. What they all have in common is they recycled the still serviceable running gear from a Mini; what a great concept!

Gordon Murray
Shalford, Surrey

Gordon Murray (left) and Jeroen Booij with the IGM Minbug.

Introduction

If I had known how much work it would take to make this book, it's possible I would never have begun. Fortunately, I was oblivious to the scale of the job when I started looking at the first of the 58 cars featured. It opened an Aladdin's cave of obscure motoring paraphernalia that was so intriguing I became insatiable for more, and there was plenty to be discovered.

According to *Cars and Car Conversions* magazine the very first Mini derivative was born in 1960, "When a keen lad whose name we can't remember turned up at, we think, Silverstone with an enterprising, but ugly, two-seater sports car based on the dear old Mini. This was a one-off, a private venture with no thoughts of series production." The *CCC* correspondent never saw it again, but the market for Mini-based cars soon exploded. GTs, coupés, roadsters and fun cars; the Mini proved to be a terrific base for some of the world's most imaginative vehicles. The subject actually proved to be so vast, this book could have had three times as many vehicles featured in it on three times as many pages. I had to draw the line. Which cars would make it and which wouldn't? I decided to leave out all the three-wheeled variants, as well as the look-alike Mini Mokes and commercials. Even then, there were still more cars than would ever fit onto 128 pages, so I relied on my own taste.

Some Mini derivatives proved to be more difficult to research than others. Sometimes I nearly gave up, until some new light was thrown on the particular car and I'd start digging again. 'Discovering' cars like the Zagato Mini Gatto or ESAP Minimach were personal breakthroughs, as were finding the most wonderful pictures unravelling the history of cars like the Gitane GT, the Butterfield Musketeer, the Coldwell GT and Pellandini. I went to Japan twice to see private collections, and was lucky to speak to many of the people who were originally involved in building or designing these cars. Craig Watson was a massive help, photographing most of the Australian Mini derivatives. He surprised me by approaching the subject with the same kind of fascination that I have. Craig, too, just didn't stop when it seemed there was no more information to be found. Thanks to him this book features such cars as the Bulanti Mini, and the Broadspeed GT that wasn't built by Ralph Broad. Cheers mate!

Something I came across while researching these fascinating little cars, apart from their Mini-motorisation, was their lack of success. Hardly any of these cars ever made money. The majority left their originators bankrupt, the illusion of becoming a motoring manufacturer ripped away. However, very often the pieces would be picked up by the next person with a dream, once again putting all their money and effort into the project. For me these personal stories are the backbone to this book and I hope you will enjoy them. The stories are exactly the reason why I would love to learn more about the cars that keep on haunting me. There still are a few mystery motors that you will find in the last chapter – perhaps they will make it into a second edition of this book; call it the Mk2.

Jeroen Booij
Amsterdam

Autocars Marcos

Autocars was an assembly plant in Haifa, Israel, which had a contract with Standard-Triumph from 1965. When BMC became British Leyland and took over Standard-Triumph in 1968, co-founder Yitzhak Shubinski, who masterminded Autocars, decided to try his luck. Shubinski desperately wanted more popular cars in his portfolio, as most of the Standard-Triumphs were too upscale for the local market. His wish was to assemble or build the Mini in Israel. Newly-formed British Leyland was, at that time, thinking of assembling fibreglass Minis abroad, and so Shubinski's call was well timed. Political tension, however, had its effect, and during 1969 the Israelis were kindly advised to approach Marcos Cars for a solution. Marcos boss Jem Marsh flew to Israel in late 1969 where he found the works "A shambles, with little apparent concern for work or production targets," but nevertheless he signed a contract. British Leyland claimed the car would not be using the Mini name or copying its appearance. Marcos agreed with Shubinski that the car was to have a monocoque body, use the Mini's mechanicals and have a maximum weight of 700 kilograms.

Back in England, Marcos Cars started working on four prototypes with estate bodies. Rory McMath, who at that time worked for Marcos Cars, remembers the vehicles being referred to as Marcos 'W90s,' where the 'W' was

specification

Car	Autocars Marcos 'W90' and 'W95'
Wheels driven	Front
Built	Westbury (GB)
Years	1969-1970
Number	6 (4 estates; 2 fastbacks)
Featured car	Kazuo Maruyama (J)

informally known to have stood for 'Wogwagon'! Once the cars were finished they were taken to MIRA's proving ground in Nuneaton for several specific tests required by the Israeli government, with whom a contract had just been signed; two cars were shipped to them. Autocars was given a development budget of 300,000 Israeli pounds (approximately 1.2 million US dollars). British Leyland confirmed the delivery of 500 engine and suspension kits within 1970, but trouble started in February of that year when the Israeli tax system was drastically changed; the 998-engined Minis were suddenly to become very expensive. Nevertheless, in June 1970, Autocars asked Marcos to build another two prototypes with fastback bodies. The cars – called W95 – were shorter and now came with a sloping rear and hatchback door. One was shipped to Israel, but by the time it arrived Autocars' contract with the government had been declared void. Shubinski still hoped for production, but came into conflict with the rest of the management. This, along with the

contract failure, led to the downfall of Autocars, and the company was taken into receivership in October 1971.

In the early eighties the second 'W95' was photographed in a Tel Aviv kindergarten by Autocars historian Yohay Shinar, but it disappeared soon after. One of the estates was used for years by Jem Marsh's wife, Judith, before it ended up in Japan; it is probably the only Israeli Mini Marcos now remaining.

Biota Mk1

The idea for the Biota was conceived when John Houghton had a Mini-powered Midget racer built. The ungainly car was nicknamed 'The Black Lawnmower,' but Houghton loved it. He started playing with the idea of a Mini-based open roadster and soon sketched the Biota – 'Bi' meaning two, as it had two seats, and 'iota' for small, due to its size. An aluminum body prototype was built using a steel spaceframe chassis with all Mini mechanicals fitted to it, and was first shown at the Racing Car Show in January 1968, attracting quite a stir.

Houghton, who had yet to start production, teamed up with Bill Needham of Coldwell Engineering (see Coldwell GT), based in nearby Sheffield, and formed Houghton Coldwell Limited. Houghton had plans to sell 100 cars in 1969, but Needham never liked the car, he said recently.

specification

Car	**Biota Mk1**
Wheels driven	**Front**
Built	**Dinnington (GB)**
Years	**1968-1972**
Number	**25**
Featured car	**Peter Niessen (NL)**

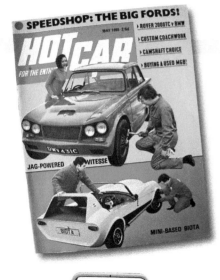

A mould was taken from the prototype body by Specialised Mouldings Limited, although this proved rather difficult due to its complicated shape. Bodies consisted of 22 fibreglass parts; the bonnet being the largest. Also, the frame proved expensive, taking a welder about five days to complete one. However, by late 1968 Houghton had rented facilities in Dinnington to start life as a true motor manufacturer. Staff were hired to weld the frames and assemble the cars, and Stewart Smith became the Managing Director. Nevertheless, it took a long time before production got off the ground and, as a result, the company began offering all kinds of fibreglass devices to earn some money; from fishing baskets to bolt-on aerodynamic front- and rear-ends for the Mini. It was not until the summer of 1970 that the first Biota was delivered. The price for a basic kit was £250, and an assembled car with a reconditioned 998cc Cooper engine was £650. Some cars went abroad after the Biota went on show in Amsterdam.

According to one member of the workforce Houghton was not the easiest man to work with. He soon parted company from Needham, and had arguments with Stewart Smith all the time; they decided to split the business in two. Houghton

Development Ltd would be used for the cars, and Biota Products for all the other fibreglass goods; Houghton led the former, Smith the latter.

John Houghton continued to race and had some success with his blue 1275cc Cooper-powered Biota. In 1972 Chris Seaman won the BARC Hillclimb Championship in it. Houghton came third in the car when it was entered again in the same competition. By this time, 25 Mk1s had been built.

Biota Mk2

After 25 Biota Mk1s had been built John Houghton decided it was time to redesign the car, and introduced the Mk2. The new car no longer had the one-piece lift-off bonnet with removable central bulge. Instead, it was replaced with a complete hinge-forward bonnet to give easier engine access, with the front featuring a larger grille and rounder edges. Even more changes were found in the spaceframe chassis. The main objection to the Mk1 had been the very narrow bench, so Houghton decided to widen the frame so proper seats could be fitted. It was now also easier to get in the car as the sills had been lowered. The rear of the chassis was changed so De Dion-type rear suspension with four-link

location could be fitted, and a new bucket seat called a Clam Seat, which featured an integral headrest and an extra cushion, was available. After winning the 1972 BARC Hillclimb Championship in the Mk1, Houghton's hillclimb car was modified into a Mk2 and also featured in advertisements. A member of the Biota crew remembers taking the car to the hillclimb events on the back of the works VW Transporter where Houghton picked it up, having driven to the venue in his Porsche 912. Houghton's crew also built another Mini-engined Midget racer, which Houghton raced under the Biota banner to promote the new 'Formula Mini-class', although this never really got off the ground.

specification

Car	**Biota Mk2**
Wheels driven	**Front**
Built	**Dinnington (GB)**
Years	**1972-1974**
Number	**6**
Featured car	**Michael Bax (NL)**

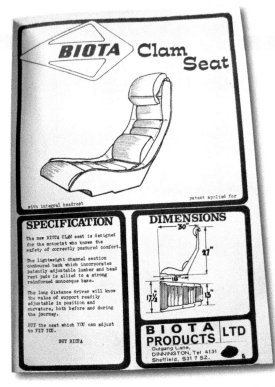

BIOTA Clam Seat

with integral headrest   patent applied for

SPECIFICATION

The new BIOTA CLAM seat is designed for the motorist who knows the safety of correctly postured comfort.

The lightweight channel section contoured back which incorporates patently adjustable lumber and head rest pads is allied to a strong reinforced monocoque base.

The long distance driver will know the value of support readily adjustable in position and curvature, both before and during the journey.

BUY the seat which YOU can adjust to FIT YOU.

BUY BIOTA

DIMENSIONS

BIOTA PRODUCTS LTD

Outgang Lane, DINNINGTON, Tel 4131 Sheffield, S31 7 SZ.

Biota Mk2

Although the Biota was a better car in Mk2 guise, it proved to be less popular than the Mk1 and only six had been built by 1974. Houghton had made plans for a hardtop version with doors, and a hatchback, too, but these cars never saw the light of day. There was also an idea for the Biota CA – a shooting brake sports car that could be fitted with a much more powerful engine from the likes of BLMC to Porsche; a model was made, but the car never saw production.

Tired of the Biota project Houghton sold everything to mini racer Jeff Williamson, but no more cars were ever built. It is believed that the moulds eventually ended up in the possession of an Argentinean, who had plans to use them to make a golf cart! The red car pictured here (chassis number HC2X41-6-74) is the sixth Mk2 and the very last Biota built. It comes with a 998cc Cooper engine, Clam Seats, and has never been road-registered.

Boro GT

While there are some home-built cars featured in this book, the majority of DIY jobs haven't been included, despite the sheer number of 'specials' that existed in the days when wrecked Minis were as cheap as chips.

The Boro GT, however, is a great exception. It was built by Robin Lacey and his father, Eric, who spent two years in the latter's 'Borough Garage' in Hedon, Yorkshire. The Boro was built up from two Mini subframes, joined together by a spaceframe made from square tubing. The floors were sheet steel, but the bodywork was nearly all aluminium, all hand-beaten, and gas welded by the Laceys. The bonnet turned out to be the most difficult part to make, but luckily Robin and Eric discovered that an old Hillman Minx bonnet fitted

perfectly. An 850cc Mini engine was bored out to 890cc, and an Aquaplane cylinder head was fitted, as were twin Stromberg carburettors. The interior was trimmed professionally in black vinyl.

With a height of just 42 inches the car was very low, and the wheelbase just two inches longer than that of the original Mini. The Lamborghini Miura-style rear window slats gave the engine some extra cooling – a radiator was fitted at the rear of the car, cooled by air drawn from the rear vents.

BIRTHDAY TREAT IS D-I-Y SPORTS CAR

ROBIN LACEY, of Hedon, will be 17 tomorrow and old enough to drive. And waiting for him is a sleek yellow sports job with a top speed of 100mph.

And there's something even more special about the car. He built it himself.

After two years of hard work —and a great deal of help from his father—the car was finished a few weeks before his birthday.

Robin, of Borough Garage, Sheriff Highway, Hedon, said today "I'll fit 'L' plates tonight and take her out for a quick spin tomorrow. I'm going to arrange driving lessons later."

Robin had wanted a sports car for a long time, and after studying many designs with his father, Mr Eric Lacey, they decided on their own style.

The finished product resembles a Lotus Europa at the front and is fitted with a Mini's reconditioned engine. The body is hand-shaped beaten aluminium, and the black interior, designed by the Laceys, was fitted by some of Robin's friends.

Since its completion Mr Lacey senior has been driving the car and has already clocked 1,200 miles.

"I must admit it's a very nice piece of work," he said. "I like it so much that I'm seriously thinking of building another for myself."

Robin Lacey's new sports car.

specification

Car	**Boro GT**
Wheels driven	**Rear**
Built	**Hedon (GB)**
Years	**1970**
Number	**1**
Featured car	**Robin Lacey (USA)**

The Boro was finished and given to Robin just before his 17th birthday, whereupon it was featured in the local newspaper as recognition of this extraordinary birthday gift. Eric told the local press: "I must admit it's a very nice piece of work. I like it so much that I am seriously thinking of building another for myself."

Robin drove the car in and around Hedon for years. Originally it was painted bright orange, but at some stage Robin decided to change it to Metal Flake Blue, in keeping with the fashion of the day. Eric didn't like the new paint job at all, and decided to have the car repainted again; this time to red. By the time Eric Lacey passed away in the late nineties, Robin had moved to the United States to start his own motor accessory company. He has thought of transporting the Boro GT to America, but as yet, the car remains in the family garage in Hedon.

Broadspeed GT 2+2

From the early sixties, Birmingham-based Broadspeed was famous for its Mini racing team, and had a great reputation as a tuning company. In February 1966 Broadspeed boss Ralph Broad unveiled a car under his own name: the Broadspeed GT 2+2. *Cars and Car Conversions* was the first to test-drive it, writing: "This is more the ultimate in conversion than a complete new car."

The design of the car came from Broadspeed's sales manager, Tony Bloor. The transformation was done by cutting the rear section off the body of a standard Mini (not a Van), and reducing the height of the door pillars by about two inches to lower the roofline. Next, a fibreglass fastback was bonded to the car and body panels, and the roof gutter deseamed. Finally, the engine was tweaked to Broadspeed specifications; all in all a pretty tough job, and not cheap either.

Broadspeed offered four versions, of which the lightweight GTS was the ultimate. Prices were on demand, but a standard GT 2+2 with a 998cc Cooper engine started at £905. The interior was changed drastically from the Mini, featuring a new fascia and many extra switches, lights and auxiliary gauges. Restall buckets and a unique rear seat were fitted, the latter could be folded down to gain access to the luggage compartment as the boot lid no longer existed. The new rear made the car about four inches longer than the standard Mini, and featured a Kamm-tail with spoiler, quick release filler cap, and rear lights from a Singer Gazelle.

specification

Car	**Broadspeed GT 2+2**
Wheels driven	**Front**
Built	**Birmingham (GB)**
Years	**1966-1968**
Number	**28**
Featured car	**Yukitoshi Yamada (J)**

Autocar described it as: "Masquerading as a sort of scaled down DB6 Aston Martin"; comments that Ralph Broad must have appreciated.

Although there was the GTS racing version the car was mainly aimed at the luxury market. The prototype exhibited at the Olympia was to be given away in a newspaper competition, but the eventual winner opted for cash, instead. John Fitzpatrick and Tony Bloor raced the car, but after a few outings it was sold to Tonio Hildebrand of the Netherlands, who continued racing it at Zandvoort. With a 1366cc Cooper engine it had a claimed top speed of 140mph, and an estimated price of about £2000.

In 1968 Broadspeed's racing team switched from the Mini to the Ford Escort; BMC was not amused. Ralph Broad decided to stop production of the car when, in 1968, his premises in Birmingham were to be demolished for a new ring road. By that time, 28 GTs had been built, 16 of which were reputedly exported to Spain.

Broadspeed GT (by Brian Foley)

I n November 1963, British racing ace John Fitzpatrick was 'Down Under' competing for the BMC Works team in the Sandown International Six Hour race; it was here that he teamed up and became friends with Brian Foley (pictured with driver armband). Foley, also a racer, had a garage in New South Wales, mainly selling used Minis. When Foley visited the UK in early 1966 Fitzpatrick introduced him to Ralph Broad, where, in his Birmingham workshop, Foley saw the Broadspeed GT and immediately became infatuated. Broad liked the idea of exporting his cars, so together they decided that Foley would become the Australian Broadspeed importer. Back in Australia, however, Foley's business partner Laurie Stewart calculated that it would be cheaper to build the cars locally than to import them. Ralph Broad granted them licence to build the car, and sent one over to Foley's workshop to have a mould made.

Like the English Broadspeed, the Australian equivalent was offered in four variants. The base model 2+2 derived from the Australian 998 Mini De Luxe, while the 2+2 S and 2+2 Super De Luxe versions were based on the Australian Cooper S.

specification

Car	**Broadspeed GT**
Wheels driven	**Front**
Built	**Caringbah (AUS)**
Years	**1967**
Number	**4**
Featured car	**Barry Dare (AUS)**

Broadspeed GT (by Brian Foley)

The latter came with a new dashboard layout, centre console, bucket seats and extra soundproofing. The fourth variant was the GTS lightweight racer. Across the four versions, prices varied from $2930 to $3390 AUD.

Compared to the English versions, there were some significant differences to those based on the Australian Minis. Doors on the Aussie Broadspeeds had wind-up windows and quarter vents, standard Mini rear lights and a small number plate recess to fit the Australian number plate. The interior on the base models remained pretty much unchanged from the standard Mini, apart from on the Super de Luxe, which was very luxurious.

Only one GTS was built, extensively raced by Laurie Stewart. It even set a record at Bathurst when clocked on Conrod Straight at 127.8mph. It was later converted to a road car and became just one of four Australian Broadspeed GTs. The car was not the success Broad and Foley had hoped for. The GTS still exists, as does the 2+2 Super De Luxe featured here; the whereabouts of the other two cars is unknown. There are some Broadspeed replicas in Australia; a company called Roadworks Design in Queensland offered a replica roof in the mid-eighties.

Buckle Monaco

By 1966 the Mini was hugely popular all over the world. In Australia, for example, the cars were built under licence, and a number were also converted there. The best-known conversion is the Buckle Monaco (sometimes called Mini Monaco). The man who came up with the idea was Bill Buckle, a BMC agent in Brookvale who had already been involved in motor manufacture. His dream of building an all-Australian sports car started in the mid-fifties with the Buckle Coupé. Although not many of these pretty cars were built, Buckle did have success with his next project, the Goggomobil Dart. It was a tiny roadster based on chassis and mechanicals from the German Goggomobil micro car; with around 700 produced, the Dart became a bestseller.

In 1966, Buckle announced the Monaco conversion. For AU $400 you could have your standard Mini or Mini Cooper converted into a sleek coupé, featuring a fibreglass roof produced from polycarbonate and extra hoops for additional support. The rear screen was also polycarbonate, while the side screens were Perspex. The standard Mini front screen was raked back to give the body better aerodynamics. All in all the Monaco was four inches shorter in height than a standard Mini. Naturally it had less headroom, so the front seats were inclined and the steering column lowered to

specification

Car	**Buckle Monaco**
Wheels driven	**Front**
Built	**Brookvale (AUS)**
Years	**1966-1967**
Number	**Approximately 30**
Featured cars	**John Centrone (AUS); Col Wickens (AUS)**

compensate. For an extra AU $200 the Mini would be equipped with wooden dashboard, aluminium wheels, leather-bound steering wheel, black vinyl interior, and a grille with fog and driving lamps.

Of the approximated 30 Monacos built, the majority were based on the Australian-built Mini Cooper S. Surviving examples are scarce; the black car pictured here, based on a Cooper S, was restored over a fifteen-year period by its current owner. The racer in Castrol livery is known as the

Buckle LMS (Lakis Manticas Special). Built from an Australian Cooper S, wrecked at Oran Park by racing driver Lakis Manticas, it is one of the lightest Minis ever to have raced the Australian tracks.

Bulanti Mini

During his time working for Nota Engineering (see Nota Fang), Brian Rawlings had seen how to build a sports car. Upon working for himself, it wasn't too much of a surprise when he devised his own sports car. Rawlings' workshop was christened Bulant Motors and located next to Amaroo Park raceway in New South Wales, where track testing wasn't too much of a hassle. Several racing specials were built there, of which the first two were powered by Morris 8 engines.

In 1971, Rawlings came up with his first road car, a two-seater sports car named Bulanti, with added 'i' to make it sound Italian. A Mini engine was positioned in a tubular spaceframe behind the seats, while an ordinary Mini subframe was found at the front. Wheelbase, track, length and width were all similar to a Mini saloon, but the overall proportions of the car were very different. With a rounded-off front and back, relatively long nose, square headlights just above the front wheels (sourced from a Hillman Hunter), and very short overhang at the rear, the car looked very sporty indeed. The downside was the closed coupé body, making access to the engine rather limited, to say the least; requiring you to crawl over the two seats to remove a panel placed over the engine. In addition to the engine, suspension and steering, Mini parts were used on the interior as well as the exterior. The doors were made by Bulant, but featured all the Mini's fittings: handles, hinges and cut down windows. However, the windscreen was

specification

Car	**Bulanti Mini**
Wheels driven	**Rear**
Built	**Annangrove (AUS)**
Years	**1971**
Number	**3**
Featured car	**Henry Draper (AUS)**

sourced from a Triumph Herald. The prototype body was hand-beaten in aluminium, but it was Rawlings' intention to build his Bulanti in a series with fibreglass bodies, so a mould was made.

Rawlings managed to sell two cars, building them with slightly different chassis, using more sheet metal instead of tubing. However, when he found out how demanding his customers were – one even asking for an ashtray to be fitted – Rawlings soon decided he had had enough of the project and brought it to an end. The car pictured on these pages is the aluminium prototype; the whereabouts of the other two 'production cars' are unknown.

Butterfield Musketeer

When Richard Butterfield watched Minis racing at Brands Hatch in 1960 he had a refreshingly new idea; why not put a two-seater GT body on one? The 21-year-old decided to give up his horticultural study and set up Butterfield Engineering in his father's Dovecroft Nursery in Nazeing, Essex. Together with his friend, Francis Manning, they produced a ⅛-scale model of their idea, and also a plywood jig. Bodywork manufacturer Williams & Pritchard had previously made an aerodynamic nose section for Richard's Triumph TR3, and was now given the job of building a prototype aluminium body for the Musketeer. The two-seater coupé

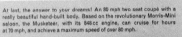

THE G.T. MINI IS HERE!

At last, the answer to your dreams! An 80 mph two seat coupé with a really beautiful hand-built body. Based on the revolutionary Morris-Mini saloon, the Musketeer, with its 848cc engine, can cruise for hours at 70 mph, and achieve a maximum speed of over 80 mph.

IT COMBINES ELEGANCE, LUXURY & PERFORMANCE

BUTTERFIELD ENGINEERING presents

THE MUSKETEER OFFERS YOU ALL THIS!
* 80 mph plus performance
* Disc brakes
* The revolutionary new Morris-Mini power pack
* Luxurious interior, adjustable bucket seats, and fantastic luggage space
* Windscreen washers, light alloy steering wheel and full instrumentation as standard equipment

850 & 1000 VERSIONS OF

The Musketeer

DOVECROFT WORKS, PAYNES LANE, NAZEING, ESSEX

specification

Car	**Butterfield Musketeer**
Wheels driven	**Front**
Built	**Nazeing (GB)**
Years	**1961-1962**
Number	**3**
Featured car	**–**

bodywork was finished just in time to have the car assembled for the Racing Car Show of January 1962. Both men had retained as much of the Mini's original mechanicals as possible. Butterfield: "I wanted to take advantage of the handling characteristics and simplicity of the original car. Simplicity was important because I had only limited engineering experience." The Mini's subframes were joined together by two longitudinal tubes with welded crossmembers. The front engine configuration was retained, but moving the radiator to the front of the car gave it a relatively low nose. The complete front section could be tilted forwards for easy engine access.

The aluminium prototype came with an 850cc engine, giving the Musketeer a top speed of 80mph. The planned production cars would have fibreglass bodies, and be offered with the option of a Cooper 1000cc engine. Prices started at £848 for the Musketeer 850, while the Musketeer 1000 came in at £892. There was a tailor-made interior with hinged seats allowing access to the rear luggage compartment, housing a spare wheel and tool kit. Soon after the show, the prototype was

stripped and returned to Williams & Pritchard so moulds could be manufactured.

In the end, only two fibreglass bodies were made; one went to a company in Portsmouth, while the other became the prototype for a twin-engined version, although this was never completed. The original aluminium prototype was rebuilt with a Mini Cooper engine and entered into the Peco Trophy race at Brands Hatch on Boxing Day 1962. Well-known Mini racer Christabel Carlisle drove the car during the event, competing against no less then eight Lotus Elites, and many other faster machines. Unfortunately, Carlisle spun the Musketeer during the race and did not finish.

Lack of experience and insufficient funds forced Richard Butterfield to wind down his engineering company; it is unknown what happened to the three cars. He moved to the United States in 1975 and took his modified Triumph TR3 with him. After 50 years he still owns it, but says: "It is overdue for a major restoration!"

Camber GT

It was in Camber Sands, Surrey, that George Holmes ran an agricultural engineering business selling lawnmowers and maintaining them for green keepers at nearby golf courses. However, in 1966 Holmes' life changed when he also became a motoring manufacturer. His friend, Derek Bishop, from southeast London, had previously built the Heron Europa sports car and was looking for a new challenge; he persuaded Holmes to cooperate.

Together they penned a mini-based GT with a front-mounted engine, and started building a prototype body in Greenwich. Upon completion it was taken over to Camber Sands to fit the mechanicals, the location subsequently providing its name, the Camber GT.

Construction was strong; a tubular steel frame with Mini subframes front and rear, fibreglass body, and reinforced with steel in the roof. The strong, fibreglass body shell had three layers and could be painted white, pale blue, red or Fiesta Yellow, although other colours were available at extra costs. Prices for a body shell started at £260; the design was pretty in its simplicity. The Camber's bonnet was made relatively low as Holmes and Bishop had repositioned the Mini's side-mounted radiator to the front of the car.

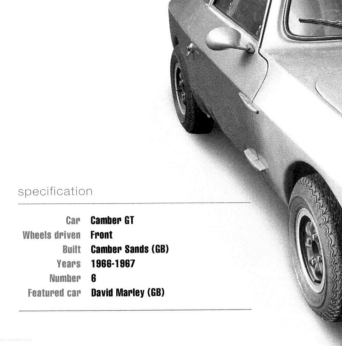

specification

Car	**Camber GT**
Wheels driven	**Front**
Built	**Camber Sands (GB)**
Years	**1966-1967**
Number	**6**
Featured car	**David Marley (GB)**

	CASTROL	BP	ESSO	MOBIL	SHELL
ENGINE/ TRANSMISSION UNIT, OILCAN, CARBURETTORS	CASTROLITE	SUPER VISCO- STATIC	ESSO EXTRA MOTOR OIL	MOBILOIL SPECIAL 10W/30	SHELL SUPER MOTOR OIL
GREASE POINTS	CASTROLEASE LM	ENERGREASE L2	ESSO MULTI-PURPOSE GREASE H	MOBILGREASE MP	SHELL RETINAX A
UPPER CYLINDER LUBRICANT	CASTROLLO	UPPER CYLINDER LUBRICANT	ESSO UPPER CYLINDER LUBRICANT	MOBIL UPPERLUBE	SHELL UPPER CYLINDER LUBRICANT

CAMBER CARS LTD. RYE, SUSSEX, ENGLAND. RECOMMENDED LUBRICANTS

CHASSIS NO. 669 A 103 ENGINE NO.

Holmes and Bishop exhibited the Camber GT at the 1967 Racing Car Show in London, and soon after that signed an agreement with Checkpoint Limited, an accessory company that was to market and distribute the vehicle. However, they eventually found out the headlights were placed too low to meet regulations, requiring the front of the car to be modified (see Maya GT). Bishop became unhappy with Checkpoint, and eventually retracted from the Camber project.

Only six Cambers were built, and from those only one car had a lightweight shell with two laminated layers. This car was sold to photographer John D Green, who raced it intensively in the year and a half he owned it; he sold it in 1968 to finance his next racing project. The silver-grey car on these pages is the lightweight Camber that has now been in the possession of its second owner for four decades.

Coldwell GT

O f all the Mini derivatives in this book the Coldwell GT is not only one of the most radical, it is one of the least known, too. This extremely low car was designed and built by racing engineer Bill Needham, who had a workshop at Coldwell Lane in Sheffield, hence the car's name. Needham had previously been involved with tuning Lotuses, but in 1967 he became the first to develop and build a racing Mini with a revolutionary twin-cam A-series engine.

The Coldwell GT saw the light of day at the Racing Car Show in January 1969 and had been engineered with the same kind of precision as the twin-cam engine. A race car with no compromises, its chassis was built up from a multitude of round steel tubes and came with full independent suspension, using double wishbones and coil springs all round. The fibreglass coupé bodywork had tiny doors, making it very difficult to get into

specification

Car	**Coldwell GT**
Wheels driven	**Rear**
Built	**Sheffield (GB)**
Years	**1969**
Number	**4**
Featured car	**Kazuo Maruyama (J)**

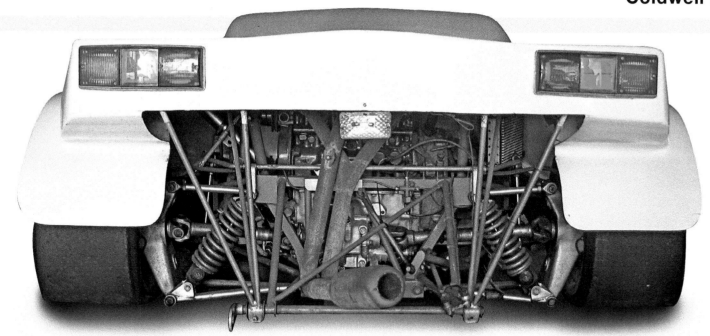

the car, and the Mini engine was mounted at the rear, just behind the driver; this was a car destined to race, and that was exactly what it did. The lightweight GT beat some of the more powerful cars of the late sixties and early seventies. At some point during 1969 his twin-cam Mini engine was fitted to the car, but Needham later swapped it for a more conventional Cooper S engine.

It was through his racing escapades that Needham found customers for the car. His own racer – the first Coldwell GT built – was bought in early 1970 by a man who took it to Singapore to race. It was entered into the 1970 Macau Grand Prix in November and came sixth, although Needham supposes the car was later crashed; the man sent him a letter asking: "Can you repair this part?" accompanied by a picture of the car with a circle drawn around the complete front end! Needham never heard anything more, and so assumes the car still resides in Singapore.

The second car built was found in a derelict state during the early eighties. With Needham's help it was restored, before being sold to the Maruyama collection in Japan. The third car is believed to have ended up in an American museum, while the fourth and last Coldwell GT,

never finished and thought lost for decades, was found by Needham in a Sheffield garage in 2007; he now plans to complete it after all these years.

Cox GTM

Although the GTM is no longer built, the company GTM is still in business building 'unspoilt sports cars.' It began in 1966 when Jack Hosker made a model for a GTM (Grand Touring Mini); it is believed he made the chassis model from packets of cornflakes. Fortunately for him, his friend Bernard Cox, who ran the garage Cox & Co in Hazel Grove, Cheshire, liked the model, and offered Hosker a corner within his premises to build a prototype, which he did just in time to unveil the Cox GTM at the Racing Car Show of January 1967.

The car was built up as a semi-monocoque made of sheet steel with a box-section backbone, Mini front subframes front and rear, and a fibreglass

The chassis is of Semi Monocoque construction, made up from different thicknesses of sheet steel electrically spot welded and riveted giving high strength weight ratio, resulting in a light but very strong structure.

specification

Car	Cox GTM
Wheels driven	Rear
Built	Hazel Grove (GB)
Years	1967-1968
Number	55
Featured car	Stuart Poole (GB)

body. The Mini engine was fitted to the rear subframe, making the GTM the first mid-engined kit car. Under the forward-tilting bonnet you could find the radiator and standard Mini petrol tank. The Cox GTM was offered as a kit only, but a body/chassis unit could also be ordered for £330. The prototype was fitted with a 1293cc engine, and was raced during the 1967 season by racing enthusiast Howard Heerey, who worked at a nearby garage and helped test the prototype.

For the 1968 season, Heerey and Cox built a new, lighter racing car that came with a 1150cc engine. The car received great promotion and praise when *Cars and Car Conversions* magazine tested an early Cox GTM: "It's nearly all Mini – and it don't 'arf go!" The testers managed to accelerate from 0-60mph in 6.4 seconds, reporting a top speed of 115.5mph. The magazine's editor subsequently built his own GTM and reported the building process in the magazine. He later raced the car around the UK, and even entered it into the Nürburgring 500 kilometres in September 1970. By that time, Bernard Cox had given up production of the vehicle for nearly two years. Howard Heerey and his father, Brian, took over production of the GTM in 1968. They made some changes to the design, replacing the Mini front subframe at the rear with a spaceframe. It is believed only 55 Cox GTMs were built. Under the Heerey name another 170 GTMs were produced between 1969 and 1970; the production rights were later sold several times (see GTM Coupé).

DART

There is only one DART – probably the most famous of all Mini derivatives; the popular Mini Marcos, Mini Jem, and also the Kingfisher Sprint were all born from it. The car was initiated in 1963 by Desmond 'Dizzy' Addicott, who liked the Mini and started playing with the idea of modifying and streamlining it for racing. Addicott, a fighter pilot, and regular Mini racer in his spare time, christened his project DART (Dizzy Addicott Racing Team). Help came from Paul Emery, who built, engineered and maintained racing cars from his west London workshop. The two men bought a damaged Morris Mini Van and started work, cutting off the roof, sectioning the windscreen and front wings to reduce the frontal area, and making a new sloping back with a cut-off Kamm tail. As a pilot, Addicott wanted to use lightweight materials, but the car was eventually made of steel. A 1071cc Cooper engine with redesigned rocker cover was fitted, only just allowing it to fit under the bonnet. The car was tested in a wind tunnel where it proved to be very aerodynamic and stable.

At the Racing Car Show in London in January 1964 the DART was shown officially on Paul Emery's stand. Just like Addicott, Emery had

specification

Car	**DART**
Wheels driven	**Front**
Built	**Send (GB)**
Years	**1964**
Number	**1**
Featured car	**Stefan Wray (GB)**

just launched his own car – the pretty Hillman Imp-based Emery GT – the little stand was good for two world premieres! The DART was well received and Addicott made plans for production. The idea was to make a fibreglass monocoque body structure and market it as a kit. With the steel prototype as a model, a mould was made with the help of Jem Marsh, of Marcos fame.

A few fibreglass bodies were eventually produced, but apparently Addicott was not happy with the quality of the shells. Disagreements followed and Addicott and Marsh went their separate ways. In just under a year Marsh had developed the project which lead to the Mini Marcos. Addicott, having had enough of the DART project, sold it to Jeremy Delmar-Morgan, who turned it into the Mini Jem in 1966.

Exactly what happened to the original steel prototype is a bit of a mystery. However, in the nineties it turned up in a Leicester scrapyard, although in very bad shape. After changing hands several times, the remains of the prototype finally ended up in the possession of its current owner who restored it beautifully; it was finished in late 2008. 'Dizzy' Addicott sadly passed away three years earlier in December 2005, at the age of 83.

Davrian Mk7

Since the first prototype was built in 1965, Davrians and their subsequent owners were always active in motor sports. To build a Hillman Imp-engined Davrian required some DIY skills, resulting in a range of cars from ultra-lightweight racers to heavyweights for forest stage rallying. However, in an effort to attract more people Davrian director Adrian Evans decided to make the car available for other engines; naturally the Mini's transverse engine was one of them.

By the time of the London Racing Car Show in January 1973 the Davrian was in its seventh guise and finally had the option of being fitted with a Mini engine. All Mini-powered Davrians came with a chassis number starting with 'DM,' for 'Davrian Mini,' with prices starting at £1085 for a rolling chassis.

Compared to its Imp-based brothers the DM hadn't changed that dramatically.

specification

Car	**Davrian Mk7**
Wheels driven	**Rear**
Built	**London/Llwynygroes (GB)**
Years	**1973-1979**
Number	**5**
Featured car	**Chris Griffiths (GB)**

It was built up from a lightweight fibreglass monocoque body, the sills and voids of which were filled with polyurethane, providing additional rigidity. Hillman Imp suspension could still be used, although Davrian's own swinging and trailing arms were also available. The car featured a one-piece flip-front with the radiator underneath, and the rear of the body was completely removable for easier access to the Mini engine, placed in a specially made subframe.

By 1976, Adrian Evans had moved from busy Clapham to rural Llwynygroes in Wales, taking the Davrian production with him. By this time, Davrians had become quite successful in many kinds of motor sports, and the company had begun running its own works team in modsports racing. Ian Hall built and raced the very first Mini-powered Davrian Mk7, and with great success, winning the 1980 BRSCC Modsports Championship outright; the car was fitted with a 1071cc Mini engine and supercharger. Legendary Mini Marcos TransXL racer Steven Roberts (see Mini Marcos Mk4/5/6) took the 1460cc engine from his famous Mini Marcos and bolted it into a Davrian Mk7, too. He raced the car under TransXL sponsorship from 1980 to 1984, and in that period drove nearly a hundred races.

Roberts' Davrian Mk7, as featured on these pages, no longer has the TransXL sponsoring, but the car is still Mini-powered and still used extensively in competition.

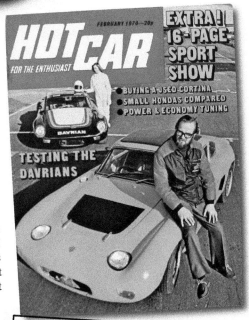

Davrian Mk8

As mentioned in the previous chapter, Adrian Evans moved Davrian production from busy London to rural Wales in late 1975. Evans had planned to move into new premises there in Felinfach, but not everything went to plan, so for a couple of years the bodies were built at his home in Llwynygroes and the cars assembled in a garage in Pontyfendigaid.

When Davrian Developments finally moved to an industrial estate in Lampeter, the Davrian Mk8 was ready for production. The model was considerably revised with a reshaped front and rear end, and it now featured an integrated radiator duct in the bonnet with square fixed cowled headlights. There was a duralumin undertray with integrated inner wheelarches and Davrian-designed disc brakes all round. A roll bar was standard, and the interior had been revised, too, with increased headroom and more facilities. However, the most important change was the engine, which was moved forward and now became mid-mounted. Most of the Mk8s were fitted with Ford Fiesta engines, but customers could also opt for a Mini-engined Mk8.

The brochure stated: "As the Davrian has outlasted the production of the original Hillman/Chrysler Imp the Davrian chassis/suspension/brakes have been built to take a wider range of engine/transmission packages. Spring rate shock absorber settings are virtually all that has to be altered to accommodate these alternatives." Prices started from £2800 in kit form.

specification

Car	**Davrian Mk8**
Wheels driven	**Rear**
Built	**Llwynygroes (GB)**
Years	**1980-1983**
Number	**5**
Featured car	**Robin Cheeseman (GB)**

Davrian Mk8

CHASSIS No. DM/8/022

DAVRIAN
Developments Ltd.
65 North Street, London, SW4

SUPPLIED TO

With backing from the Welsh Development Agency, Evans planned to sell the Mk8 for the first time as a complete car, calling it the Davrian Dragon. However, his plans didn't go as well as hoped, and Davrian Developments went into receivership in February 1983. By that time approximately 50 Mk8s had been built, of which only five were fitted with a Mini engine, and as with the Mk7s, they had a chassis number starting with 'DM' for 'Davrian Mini.' Davrian's production rights were taken over by Will Corry from Northern Ireland who updated the car and renamed it the Corry Cultra, but it proved unsuccessful. Tim Duffee took it over from Corry and changed it into a rather successful rally car, renaming it Darrian T9 in 1987. Adrian Evans passed away in 1992.

DAVRIAN

Deep Sanderson 105

In the early sixties, Mini derivatives were the trend, but the Twini was another. They were, of course, Minis with a second Mini engine in the boot driving the rear wheels! Paul Emery (see Gitane GT) reputedly built the first Twini as early as 1961, but others soon followed. Daniel Richmond and John Cooper built a Twini that BMC entered into the Targa Florio of 1963, but BMC banned the building of more twin-engined Minis after Cooper narrowly survived a crash in one; however, privateers were still tempted to continue. One such privateer was racing cyclist Reg Harris, who had the Deep Sanderson 105 built to race in sprints. Like Emery's and Cooper's Twinis it used transversely-mounted Mini engines front and rear, but came in the shape of a single-seater, with aluminium body. The car was built in late 1963 by Christopher Lawrence, with the two 1071cc Cooper engines sourced from Downton Engineering. The car used a Mini subframe at the front and a tubular frame at the rear, similar to that of the Deep Sanderson 301. As everything was doubled on the car there were many linkages operating the double clutches, throttles and gearboxes. Changing gear must have been pretty difficult, but Lawrence managed well; in his biography he writes: "I could set the throttle linkages so that the rear engine came in before the

specification

Car	**Deep Sanderson 105**
Wheels driven	**Front and rear**
Built	**London (GB)**
Years	**1963**
Number	**1**
Featured car	**Larry Webb (GB)**

Brands Hatch and displayed it on the Lawrence Tune stand at the Racing Car Show of January 1964. Lawrence raced it again in April that year at Mallory Park, although two months later he had a severe accident on his return from Le Mans (see Deep Sanderson 301), and the 105 ended up with his former F1 companion, John Pearce.

After its final outing in 1965 at Santa Pod, Pearce advertised the car in *Motor Racing* magazine, asking £975 for it. For decades the car was thought lost, only to reappear in 2007. Lawrence restored the car in 2008 and sprinted it again at the Goodwood Festival of Speed. The pictures of the car featured on these pages were taken prior to its restoration.

front one, which helped me to get the tail out for the tight corner."

Reg Harris withdrew from the project when it reached the halfway point, so Lawrence decided to have the car finished to sprint himself. He entered it unpainted for the 1963 Boxing Day Race at

Deep Sanderson 301

The first person to see the potential of placing a Mini engine at the rear of a sports car was Morgan tuner and racer Christopher Lawrence (pictured), who built a prototype for his Deep Sanderson 301 as early as 1961. Under the Deep Sanderson name (an amalgam of his father's favourite jazz song, *Deep Henderson*, and his mother's maiden name, Sanderson), Lawrence had previously built a few Formula Junior racers, but the 301 was more prestigious.

The open-top prototype was shown at the Racing Car Show in January 1962, and soon became better known as the 'Perfume Delivery Wagon' after it was pictured in a Russell Brockbank cartoon. Unfortunately, Lawrence crashed the car at the Nürburgring, but he didn't give up.

It was at the following Racing Car Show that a much better-looking, primrose yellow, aluminium coupé body prototype was exhibited. The car used a sheet metal backbone chassis, with the engine, hubs and wheels as the only Mini parts. Lawrence equipped the car with a tubular frame at the rear to mount the engine, and its 'Lawrence-Link' suspension

specification

Car	**Deep Sanderson 301**
Wheels driven	**Rear**
Built	**London/Staines (GB)**
Years	**1962-1964**
Number	**Approximately 15**
Featured car	**Christopher Lawrence (GB)**

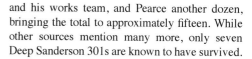

gave the car complete camber compensation to ensure the wheels always stayed upright. The aluminium body, made by Williams & Pritchard, was used to make the mould, from which the fibreglass body production cars were produced.

In 1963, a Deep Sanderson 301 was entered in the Le Mans 24-hour Race, driven by Lawrence himself and co-piloted by Chris Spender. The 998cc-powered car did well, but Spender slid the vehicle, ending up in a sandpit, causing it to be behind the minimum average time at midnight, which resulted in disqualification.

The following year Lawrence returned to Le Mans with two 1295cc-engined 301s. One was driven by Lawrence and Gordon Spice, and a second by Jim Donnely and Huw Braithwaite, who crashed it during practice. Lawrence and Spice reputedly clocked 148mph on the Mulsanne straight in their 301, but when the oil pump broke after four hours they had to give up. More bad luck occurred when Lawrence was involved in a terrible accident whilst driving his Chevrolet Corvair back home from Le Mans. He ended up in hospital for quite a while, and by the time he left, the job of building Deep Sanderson 301s had been sub-contracted to John Pearce, who built them alongside his mobile home in Staines.

It is believed Lawrence only built the 301s that were raced by him and his works team, and Pearce another dozen, bringing the total to approximately fifteen. While other sources mention many more, only seven Deep Sanderson 301s are known to have survived.

De Joux Mini GT

In addition to the United Kingdom, some tempting Mini derivatives were built abroad. Australia catered for quite a few, built from as early as 1963. New Zealand had at least one; the De Joux Mini GT. Designed and built by former McLaren engineer Ferris de Joux, it was a stunning car. However, it was not his first car; De Joux was credited to have built the first fibreglass-bodied car in New Zealand back in the late fifties. He had also made a one-off Holden GT and a one-off Buckler, as well as a Jaguar-powered Ferrari; better known as the Ferraguar.

In the summer of 1965 De Joux started playing with the idea of a Mini-based GT, with sketches appearing in *Motorman* magazine. It was a very pretty two-seater GT that used as much

specification

Car	De Joux Mini GT
Wheels driven	Front
Built	Auckland (NZ)
Years	1965-1970
Number	Approximately 20
Featured car	Warwick Robinson (NZ)

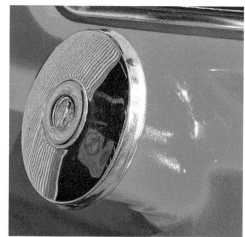

of the Mini's body and mechanicals as possible. Not only did the Mini's engine and suspension remain, but also the floorpan, bulkhead, sills and both subframes. The fibreglass body was nine inches shorter in height and two inches wider than that of a Mini. The side-mounted Mini radiator was replaced with one from a Morris Minor and relocated to the front, just behind the grille. The GT still required a small bonnet bulge to allow for the rocker cover and carburettors. Apart from all the Mini parts, the car used Austin 1100 headlights and door handles, Austin 1800 indicators, and Austin A40 door hinges, while the round rear lights were sourced from a Fiat 850 Coupé. Behind the two bucket seats was a carpeted area where one extra passenger could be accommodated. There was no exterior boot lid, but the interior boot space could be accessed via an interior flap. Kestrel Plastics of Onehunga made the bodies, while the cars were marketed by the company Fibreglass Developments, who sold them for NZ $500 each. *Motorman* magazine, first to test-drive the car in March 1970, deemed it possible to build one for approximately NZ $1700. In total, about 20 De Joux Mini GTs were built, although some are reportedly reproduced using an original body to plug a mould.

Domino Pimlico

Rust has always been one of the Mini's great weaknesses, so it wasn't particularly strange when some folks began making fibreglass body shells for the Mini. BMC attempted building plastic-bodied Mini prototypes in the mid-sixties, but the project never got off the ground in the UK. The job of building body shells was therefore left to privateers like the Status Motor Company, Minus Cars and the FRA Mini Company. Domino Cars Limited of Southampton, founded by aeronautical engineer John Chapman and GRP expert John Ingram, offered a fibreglass Mini derivative. The company formed in 1985, and by 1986 had introduced the Domino Pimlico. The Pimlico's convertible body was produced by Fibretech GRP, that also built replica Beetles named Wizard Hard Top and Wizard Roadster.

specification

Car	**Domino Pimlico**
Wheels driven	**Front**
Built	**Southampton (GB)**
Years	**1986-2007**
Number	**Unknown**
Featured car	**Ben van Leeuwen (NL)**

The Pimlico was immediately recognizable as a Mini, but was very different, too. The body was completely seamless and came with high sills, no boot lid and no doors, and a 'T-bar' (removed on the featured car). It had large incorporated wheelarches, distinctive side skirts and 'frenched' rear lights. Simple-style doors requiring external door hinges were available at extra cost, but most customers ordered their Pimlico without. The majority of cars were painted in two-tone colour schemes; some people compared it to the Ghia beach cars built on a Fiat base. The Pimlico was designed by Richard Oakes, who had worked on numerous kit cars prior to the project.

Following the success of the Pimlico the Domino range was quickly broadened. First was the Premier in 1988, with lowered door sills

that enabled double-skinned, internally hinged doors to be fitted. Next came the HT (Hard Top), the Pick-Up, and the Cabrio, all using the Mini's original steel inner door skins. The HT-ES (Hard Top/Evolution Sport) featured carbon composite instead of fibreglass, making it seriously light. Domino also built a few race shells similar to that of the HT/ES, but a spaceframe replaced the standard Mini subframes. All other Domino models came as a monocoque body, to which the Mini's standard subframes and other Mini mechanicals were fitted.

Both Domino Cars and Fibretech went into receivership in the new millennium and the assets were taken over by Domino Composites, which changed its name to Composite Designs before going into liquidation in late 2007.

Ecurie de Dez

The Australians must have loved coupé versions of the Mini. Not only did Brian Foley build an Aussie version of the Broadspeed GT in Caringbah, and Bill Buckle sell his streamlined Buckle Monaco from Brookvale, there was also the Ecurie de Dez; the brainchild of car dealer Des Higgins from Salisbury South. He was 28 years old when, in late 1968, he introduced his 2+2 coupé based on the Mini 850.

Higgins built the car in a prefabricated garage across the road from his home. He removed the roof, sectioned the centre pillars by two inches, and canted the A-pillars and windscreen by 4½ inches to give the body better aerodynamics. A fibreglass fastback roof was then fitted and the doors modified to fit under the new roofline. The front track of the car was widened by 1¾in, and

the rear suspension lowered slightly to give the car a more balanced look. Higgins also took care of the engine, modifying the head, valves, exhaust and carburettors. The first Ecurie de Dez was fitted with a 1100cc engine, and was completely rewired. Additional fog lights were fitted in the grille. The interior was completely retrimmed in black vinyl, with black perforated hood lining adding to the luxury effect. A new fibreglass fascia was fitted, as well as a centre console, complete

specification

Car	**Ecurie de Dez**
Wheels driven	**Front**
Built	**Salisbury South (AUS)**
Years	**1969-1970**
Number	**5**
Featured car	**Russell Holehouse (AUS)**

with aftermarket Smith gauges, and a rev counter and speedometer sourced from an MGB. The car was sprayed with eight coats of paint and the roof covered in black vinyl.

When the first Ecurie de Dez was finished it was displayed in the motoring pavilion at the Royal Adelaide Show in 1969, where it was very well received. It was even featured in a documentary on national television. *Sports Car World* magazine praised the car in January of that year: "It has a quality to be seen to be believed. It looks anything but a home-grown special."

Higgins built three cars on the base of Mk1 Minis while another two were made from Mk2s. After completing five cars Higgins became fed up with the project and destroyed the roof moulds. He later said: "30 years ago we didn't think anything of throwing away the moulds, but today I'm fairly disappointed with that decision."

ESAP Minimach GT

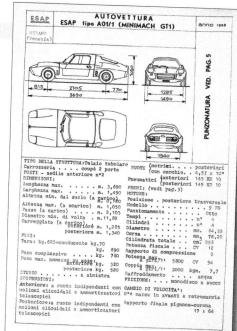

Gianfranco Padoan (pictured), from Mirano, Venice, was a keen amateur racer in the sixties, who had an accessory and tuning company called ESAP (Equipaggiamenti Sportivi Auto Preparazione). When he read about the Unipower GT in 1967 he decided he needed one, and so collected a left-hand-drive model from Universal Power Drives in England. Back in Italy, however, there were troubles with getting the car road-registered, the main problem being the lights were placed too low. This led Padoan to make

modifications to his car, resulting in a completely redesigned front and rear. The front now sported bigger rectangular headlights, and fitted Fiat 850 units at the rear. Padoan pulled up the lines above both wheelarches, and with the intention of using the car for tough motor sports, made some technical changes, the most remarkable being double springs on the rear suspension.

specification

Car	**ESAP Minimach GT**
Wheels driven	**Rear**
Built	**Mirano (I)**
Years	**1967-1968**
Number	**2**
Featured car	**Stefano Boldrin (I)**

Padoan entered the car for the 1968 Targa Florio and the Monza 1000 kilometres of the same year. By then, he had become extremely enthusiastic about the car, and decided to market it as the ESAP Minimach GT. Brochures were printed and reports written up in the Italian press. The car still looked pretty similar to the original Unipower GT, although it had been changed in various other ways. For example, the gear linkage was placed centrally instead of in the inner sill like on the Unipower. The doors were hung on outside (Mini) hinges, which meant that the bonnet had to be different, too; unlike the Unipower it tilted forwards like a Jaguar E-type. The 998cc engine was sourced from an Innocenti Mini.

Back in England, Universal Power Drives heard about the car and was not amused. According to Padoan's eldest daughter, Keti, a 14-year-long court battle followed, eventually won by her father. However, this is probably not the main reason why the Minimach never reached the production stage. The Inspettorale Generale della Motorizzazione (the Italian DVLA) proved the main obstacle; all the drawings and designs had 'Annulato' ('void') stamped on them by the authority. Keti Padoan assumes they kept her father from putting the car on the road to protect companies like Innocenti and Abarth.

Gianfranco Padoan sold ESAP after his Minimach adventure, and the company was renamed Speedline. Padoan became successful in boat-building, but died in 1996 at the age of 60. His younger daughter, Cristina, took over the boating business, now based in Florida.

Fletcher GT

When David Ogle tragically died in a car crash in May 1962 whilst driving the only Ogle Lightweight GT (see Ogle SX1000), production of his pretty Mini-based GT slowly came to an end. It was three years later when Norman Fletcher bought the moulds and remaining spares. Fletcher had a well-known boat building and supply company in Walsall, and it was his idea to keep his men occupied during the winter gap by building new racing versions of the SX1000.

The first car – now called the Fletcher GT – was finished in 1966, not differing much from

the original SX1000. It was powered by an 1149cc Cooper engine, and raced by ex-Cooper works driver John Handley that same year, coming fourth in the British Eagle Trophy Race at Brands Hatch on 27th December. It turned out there was a demand for a road version, too, and so Fletcher's team set

specification

Car	**Fletcher GT**
Wheels driven	**Front**
Built	**Walsall (GB)**
Years	**1966-1967**
Number	**4**
Featured cars	**Paul Stanworth/Paul Ogle (GB)**

themselves the task of building it. At the Racing Car Show in January 1967 the car was shown to the public, turning out to be different from the original Ogle design. The headlights were now fitted in recessed Perspex cowls, and the rear had a sharper style, featuring light clusters from the Austin 1800. It is often thought that two unused Ogle prototypes, one with a different rear and one with a different front, were part of the remaining spares that Fletcher bought, but according to several people directly involved this is not true. The restyling was done by Fletcher. After the show, orders for road-going Fletcher GTs came in from as far as Switzerland, but supply from BMC turned out to be a problem.

When interest in boats tumbled in 1967, Norman Fletcher decided to cease car production to focus solely on boat-making. Only four Fletcher GTs had been built, and none of them were the same. Only the show car had both the restyled front and rear that was also shown in Fletcher's leaflets. Although production had ceased, John Handley continued racing the first Fletcher GT during the 1967 season. He made it to the Nürburgring 500 kilometer race, qualifying the car third fastest. He was lying second in the race when, unfortunately, the engine gave up. Of the two cars shown here one is thought to be Handley's racing car, the other the Racing Car Show car.

Gitane GT

Named after the French cigarette, the Gitane GT was a very pretty car with an 887cc, 84bhp Mini engine at the rear. It was designed and built by Francophile Gordon Fowell, and backed by the Fowell family's dumper truck-building business, GF, in West Bromwich. The prototype was finished in the spring of 1962, making it one of the earlier Mini derivatives. The suspension used coil springs, but the idea was to use the Mini's original rubber springs for production versions. The prototype's beautiful body was beaten from aluminum by a retired Austin employee, and then painted a light shade of metallic green. Disc brakes were fitted, as were wire wheels, which gave no clue to its Mini-motorization. Fowell had plans to use a different engine for production cars, and made an agreement with Rome-based tuner Giannini to have more powerful engines built for the Gitanes he was considering building. First, however, he wanted to market the car by racing it in Europe, entering the sleek little GT in several races: the 1000 kilometers of the Nürburgring in May 1962, the Trophée d'Auvergne in July 1962, and even the Le Mans 24-hour Race of that year. Fowell was to drive the car himself, with London-based car dealer

IF YOU RACE A MINI CAN YOU
AFFORD TO BE WITHOUT—
THE DEALEY DIFF.
Has recorded over **150 1sts** in circuit races, sprints, hillclimbs and autocross events.
Developed for our own 1400 mini in 1966, proved throughout the 1967 season, and still running reliably on the original diff. Total successes to date are too numerous to mention.
Limited slip differential, retail price £55
Trade enquiries welcome.

specification

Car	**Gitane GT**
Wheels driven	**Rear**
Built	**West Bromwich (GB)**
Years	**1962**
Number	**1**
Featured car	**–**

LA GITANE BMC ELABORAZIONE GIANNINI

LONDRA — Dopo la Deep Sanderson un'altra vettura inglese ha adottato il motore della BMC Mini-Cooper sistemandolo posteriormente. E' il prototipo della Gitane G. T. che parteciperà a molte gare quest'anno. La produzione in serie inizierà l'anno prossimo e il suo costruttore, George Fowell, spera di equipaggiarle con un motore elaborato dall'italiano Giannini; il quale fornirà pure un nuovo cambio appositamente studiato per questa vettura. Il motore ha una cilindrata di 997 cc con un carburatore doppio corpo Weber e un rapporto di compressione di 10,2 : 1. La potenza è di 84 CV a 7800 giri/minuto e la velocità massima, a quanto dichiara il costruttore, dovrebbe aggirarsi fra i 210 e 215 km/ora. Il telaio è a

traliccio con elementi in lamiera sia anteriormente che posteriormente. La sospensione del prototipo applica le molle elicoidali mentre per la costruzione in serie è previsto il montaggio degli elementi in gomma che sono utilizzati dalla BMC 850. I freni a disco sono Girling. Ai lati del vano portabagagli che è sistemato anteriormente vi sono due serbatoi per la benzina della capacità di litri 22,5. Il radiatore si trova a fianco del motore nel retro della vettura. La carrozzeria è in alluminio e lamiera d'acciaio. Le luci di posizione sono alloggiate sul condotto d'aria per il raffreddamento dei freni a disco. Le finestre laterali posteriori sono state sostituite da griglie che permettono un miglior raffreddamento del radiatore dell'acqua e maggior accessibilità al vano motore. L'altezza della vettura è inferiore al metro.

GORDON WILKINS

Dan Margulies as a co-pilot. Margulies, however, later said he never even saw the car. Fowell drove the vehicle to France by road, but never made it to any of the intended races after losing a wheel close to Clermont-Ferrand, damaging the Gitane (above, right). One race entry was also 'not accepted.' It seems Fowell soon lost interest and sold the car.

In the mid-sixties the Gitane GT ended up in the possession of Tony 'Podge' Dealey, whose brother, Michael, initially helped Fowell to design and build it. Dealey modified the body, finding rear vision very poor. He changed the engine to a fast 1400cc unit, fitted 13in magnesium wheels, modified the gear change and painted the car red. Dealey: "It was a very robust car, and because of the weight distribution acceleration was pretty phenomenal. It was pretty high-geared, so I could do Prescott Hill in just two gears. But it used to lift a rear wheel alarmingly so I decided it needed a limited slip diff. I managed to graft a Thornton Powerlock in, which just worked. The steering was incredibly heavy, but it was virtually unbeatable. There was a great demand for the diff and I started selling them as 'The Dealey Diff,' of which I sold about 200."

Dealey sold the modified prototype Gitane minus the engine in 1968 to a chap in Devon, and it hasn't been seen since. Gordon Fowell subsequently invented the jogging machine, and made a fortune.

GTM Coupé

Jack Hosker came up with the idea for the Grand Touring Mini in 1966. Up until 1968 it saw production under several different names, originally the Cox GTM, of which 55 were made. Production sped up when Howard Heerey took over in 1968. The design of the car, now just called the GTM, changed very little, but around 170 cars were built before Howard restyled it more drastically in 1971. By that time the front had been kitted out with a low grille and spoiler that ended in a lip. A Mini front bumper was fitted, as well as new indicators

specification

Car	GTM Coupé
Wheels driven	Rear
Built	Sutton Bonnington (GB)
Years	1980-1995
Number	Approximately 500
Featured cars	Jeroen Booij (NL), Neil Weston (GB)

and sidelights; the car was now called the Heerey GTM 1-3. Approximately 70 were sold before the company was taken over in 1972 by Heglass-Fiber of Hartlepool, although in the following four years it never produced a single car, and neither did the subsequent owners, KMB Autosports, which owned the rights from 1976 to 1980.

It was in 1980 that Patrick Fitch and Peter Beck, two men with some experience in the kit car industry, thought it time to revive the GTM once again. They set up GTM Engineering and GTM Cars in rural Sutton Bonnington, Loughborough, and started working on a Grand Touring Mini for the 1980s. The car now received an even bigger front spoiler, bringing the front very low to the ground. The lines of the front lip extended around the front of the car, forming the widened wheelarches; the rear of the car received similar treatment and now featured an integral fibreglass bumper. Big light clusters were fitted at the rear, as well as a sunroof and door handles – as seen on many BL cars from the TR7 to the Range Rover. Wheels initially were 12in Cosmics, but were later changed to 13in Alleycat alloys. The interior, too, was revised completely and now came with a fibreglass 'wraparound' dashboard and armrest. By 1987 three options of kit were available, ranging from the basic Kit A at £1675 to the complete Kit C for £2620, plus VAT.

The GTM Coupé proved tremendously successful and it is believed GTM Cars sold over 500 cars between 1980 and 1995. The car was advertised regularly with: "All the essential features of an exotic Ferrari or Lotus, but at a price you can afford!"

By 1995 the company had moved on to new models, and once again the rights of the GTM Coupé were sold, this time to a company named Primo Design.

Kingfisher Sprint

Roger King was a craft teacher at a secondary school in Luton, but in the early eighties he and his wife, Christine, found it time for a radical change. He gave up his teaching job, starting a new life as a garage owner in rural Rothbury, Northumberland, repairing and maintaining Minis. However, King's ambitions stretched further than that. He'd bought an old Mini Jem Mk2 (pages 78-79), and thinking it could be improved, the idea of becoming a motoring manufacturer was born. King rented 2500ft³ of premises on the Northumberland Industrial Estate and started modifying the car, ending up with a dramatically redesigned Mini Jem. The car was six inches longer and two inches taller than the original, and had big spoilers at the front and rear. The difference in height was mainly due to a much

larger windscreen, sourced from a Volkswagen Beetle 1303. The big, flat, heated rear screen came from a Datsun 120Y Coupé, while the rear lights were sourced from a Ford Capri. The tailgate could be opened, giving access to a seriously large boot. The Mini Jem originally derived from the DART (pages 30-31), the floor of which was apparently twisted when the roof of its Mini Van base was taken off. For this reason, all the Mini Jem bodies taken from a DART mould had floors that weren't

Kingfisher Motors Limited, the new Company headed by Roger King are pleased to announce that KINGFISHER SPRINT is now in limited production. The MOTOR SHOW 1982, held at the National Exhibition Centre, Birmingham is the first showing of the production car in 2 + 2 form with the new large Hatchback and serveral detailed changes.

The car is available in any build specification from a bare bodyshell to a fully completed car. Full specification and prices are detailed overleaf.

specification

Car	**Kingfisher Sprint**
Wheels driven	**Front**
Built	**Rothbury (GB)**
Years	**1982-1984**
Number	**Approximately 35**
Featured car	**Allan Jefferey (GB)**

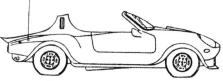

KINGFISHER CONVERTIBLE.

KINGFISHER SPRINT.

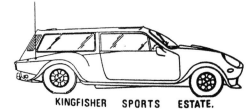

KINGFISHER FAMILY ESTATE.

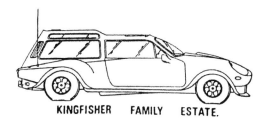

KINGFISHER SPORTS ESTATE.

Kingfisher Sprint

straight. Upon this discovery King set himself the task of straightening it; he was believed to be a perfectionist, and the car's finish was good.

Apart from the Kingfisher Sprint, a Convertible, Family Estate and Sports Estate were also planned, but these versions were never built. At £7665, King even offered a Turbosport version with a 1480cc Mini engine, complete with Rajay supercharger, giving it 125bhp. As a basic kit, the

Sprint was priced at £1144, while a complete car started at just under £4600. By late 1981, about 20 customers had ordered a Kingfisher Sprint, and the first car was officially unveiled by Lord Armstrong on January 5th 1982. It was also shown at the National Motor Show in Birmingham later that year where more orders were taken.

Perhaps it was King's perfectionism that made him lose money on the cars, or perhaps it was the wages for his three-man-strong staff, but by 1984 his company went into receivership. An attempt was made to revive it in 1985 under the name Vortex Cars, but to no avail.

Landar R6

Birmingham brothers Peter and Clive Radnall, although manufacturers of bicycle and motorcycle components, also liked a bit of racing and hillclimbing in their spare time. In 1962, seeing potential in a cheap racer, they came up with the idea to put a tuned Mini engine into the rear of a lightweight racer; it wasn't long before building started. The result was an ultra low racer (30 inches high) called the Landar R1 (based on Radnall spelt backwards). Whilst racing the car they continued to develop it to the Landar R2, R3, and so on; the final result was offered for sale in 1965 as the Landar R6.

The sleek racer had a light multi-tubular spaceframe with a Mini subframe at the rear; the former could support aluminium fuel tanks on both sides. Suspension was fully independent and adjustable front and rear. The steering column and pedals were adjustable, too, giving taller drivers the option of driving the car. Wheels were 10in steel as standard, but extra wide magnesium versions were also available. The car was offered for sale with a 1000cc Cooper engine, but could be ordered with a Broadspeed-tuned 1275, too; even a Colotti-Francior five-speed gearbox was on the options list. The wheelbase was four inches longer than that of the standard Mini, with a front/rear weight distribution of 36/64, achieved by placing the battery and spare wheel in the back. The Landar R6 prototype (below, right) had an aluminium body, but the later production cars, made by Ivory Plastics of Luton, were fibreglass. The frames for

specification

Car	**Landar R6**
Wheels driven	**Rear**
Built	**Birmingham (GB)**
Years	**1962-1970**
Number	**10**
Featured car	**Kazuo Maruyama (J)**

the first few cars were welded by the Radnalls, but eventually were sub-contracted.

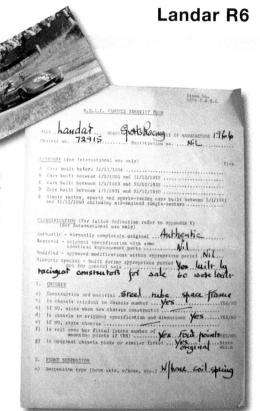

Ex-Cooper works driver John Handley tested the prototype and loved it, as did *Small Car* magazine, which was the first to test-drive it: "Steering was so gentle and progressive that the precise moment that the rear wheels started to break away could be felt and correction could be taken straight away. You could let the tail hang out just as far as you liked without getting out off hand." The basic price for the car in component form during 1965 was £945.

Although Peter Radnall is confident he and his brother built no more then ten Landar R6s, a much greater number is thought to have existed. It is believed more bodies were made after the moulds were sold in the USA; the majority of Landar R6s have ended up there, as well as in Japan.

CHASSIS/BODY

Multi-tubular space frame, constructed from ¾" and 1" round and rectangular tubing, nickel bronze welded and sprayed slate grey. Stressed monocoque side bulkheads and alloy underpay. Glass fibre body panels with "Dzus" fasteners. Drop down type doors. Full width double curvature molded perspex windscreen. **DIMENSIONS** Wheelbase 7'0": Track 50½" (front) 52½" (rear) Overall length 11'0"; Width 4'8": Height 30": Weight (approx) 855 lbs **INTERIOR** Molded glass fibre seats with top quality, black neoprene padded covers and press-stud fittings. Steering wheel is 11" diameter, covered in black hide. **INSTRUMENTS** 0-10,000 RPM electronic tachometer, oil pressure and water temperature gauges. **COLORS** Your choice, high grade spray finish. **SUSPENSION** Fully independent and adjustable for wheel camber angle. Front: adjustable spring/shock units and wide base tubular wishbones of unequal length. Rear: rubber cones, upper and lower links, radius arms, and tubular shocks. **BRAKES** 7½" discs on all four wheels. Operated by hydraulic twin master cylinders. Actuated by adjustable compensating mechanism to adjust braking ratio front/rear. **STEERING** Rack and pinion with 2½ turns lock to lock, adjustable column.

GENERAL

CAPACITIES Fuel 6 gallons. Crankcase (including transmission and filter) 5.4 qts. Radiator 3.2 qts. **FUEL SYSTEM** SU electric fuel pump (type SP) mounted in nearside monocoque section at rear of fuel tank. **FUEL TANK** Aircraft type installation, located in left front monocoque section. **LUBRICATION** Full pressure to engine bearings, sump forms oil bath for gearbox and final drive. Internal gear-type pump driven off camshaft. Full-flow oil filter with renewable element. Gauze strainer in sump. Magnetic drain plug. **COOLING** Pressurized radiator with pump. **IGNITION** 12 volt, coil and distributor.

DRIVE TRAIN

TRANSMISSION 7¼" competition diaphragm clutch, bonded and riveted disc, designed to withstand competition use. **GEARBOX** Close ratio, 4 speed, straight cut gears with 1st: 2.573; 2nd: 1.722; 3rd: 1.255; 4th: direct; Reverse: 2.573. In unit with engine and final drive. Central floor gear shift. Final drive to rear wheels via straight cut gears. Hardy spicer U-joints and open shafts. Drive casing in unit with engine and gearbox. **DIFFERENTIAL** Limited slip with your choice of 3.4; 3.7; 3.9; 4.1 final drive.

ENGINES

C/850 850cc displacement. Full race conversion using "S" type components. Provides approximately 85BHP at 8,000 RPM with 45 DCOE Weber carburetor. **C/1300** 1300cc displacement. Full race conversion from basic BMC 1275 power unit. Uses "S" type components. Approximately 120 BHP at 8,000 RPM with 45 DCOE Weber carburetor. **FI/850** Similar to C/850 but delivers 105+ BHP using fuel injection with 8 port, alloy crossflow head. **FI/1300** Similar to C/1300 but delivers 130+ BHP using fuel injection with 8 port, alloy crossflow head.

WHEELS & TIRES

6" or 8" magnesium, 10" diameter. Dunlop, Goodyear and Firestone racing compounds are available.

Landar R7

LANDAR COMPONENTS LIMITED
manufacturers of Landar cars, race engine tuning and development engineers
Dynamometer Testing Facilities 400 B.H.P. 12000 R.P.M.
4-14 DARTMOUTH STREET · BIRMINGHAM 7 · ENGLAND
telephone 021 - 359 1941 - 2

your ref.   our ref. CJR/1   date 20th May 1970.

M/s Groves Aircraft Sales Inc.
11429 Hayvenhurst Avenue,
Granada Hills,
California,
U.S.A.

Dear Sir,

By the time you get this letter you will no doubt have received
your car, before starting please check oil level, water level,
and fuel level.
Starting Procedure.
Turn on the electric isolating switch. (by drivers right hand)
Turn on ignition switch. (right hand switch)
Turn on injector pumps with throttle open for 2-3 seconds only
Push starter button, as engine starts switch pumps on, if engine
fails to start turn pumps off to avoid flooding.

Plugs : use Champion N 62 R.

Settings.
Valve Settings.
Exhaust .015)   Hot
Inlet   .015))
Static timing – set on bed. 5%   Firing order 1.3.4.2.
Contact points .014 - .016   Compression ratio 12.5-1.
                                        Head torque settings 45 lbs ft.
            Dwell 60

Continued.

Directors: P. A. RADNALL (Managing) C. J. RADNALL (Secretary)

The Landar R6 was not the success brothers Peter and Clive Radnall had hoped for, but when a new racing class for 1300s was announced for 1969 – the Firestone Formula F100 – they immediately jumped at the opportunity with a new car the Landar R7. It had to be a revolutionary new racer, and that is what it was. Unlike the R6 it did not use the Mini's engine subframe, instead the engine was bolted directly in the rear of a sophisticated spaceframe and canted forwards by twenty degrees. The R7 chassis drawings indicate this part of the design work was completed in October 1969, so the Radnalls missed the first F100 season. Unfortunately, more troubles lay ahead as the new racing class was soon to be cancelled.

However, the Landar R6 had made a small name for itself in the USA – the Radnalls had found an American distributor in John Hill, who had sold a few R6s and thought there would be a market for the R7; there was, but again it was very limited. As with the R6, the Radnalls could not build and sell the amount of cars they hoped for, and they soon ceased production of the R7.

According to Peter Radnall only four Landar R7s were built, with just the factory prototype remaining in the UK.

chassis-body specs

specification

Car	**Landar R7**
Wheels driven	**Rear**
Built	**Birmingham (GB)**
Years	**1969-1970**
Number	**4**
Featured car	**Carl Braun (USA)**

Landar r-7

The prototype was equipped with a 999cc engine, and raced by Tony Lanfranchi in the under-1000s class. The greatest competitive success the R7 had was winning the under-1300cc championship of the Sport Car Club of America.

In 1970, the brothers moved away from Birmingham, ending their car production. The last car they built was a Ford-powered two-litre Group 6 racer – the Landar R8 – but it remained a one-off. The yellow Landar R7 in these photographs was sold as new, equipped with a Cooper S engine bored to 1300cc, Weslake eight-port cross flow head, Tecalemit-Jackson fuel injection, Salisbury limited slip differential, and 13in magnesium Minilites. It was air freighted from the factory to the USA in April 1970 and has raced there ever since.

DIMENSIONS
wheelbase 90" track, front 56" track, rear 57" overall length 139" width 67" height 28" weight (with engine) approximately 850 lbs

CHASSIS
multi-tubular space-frame, 3/4" and 1" dia. steel tubing, nickel-bronze brazed, finished in slate-grey enamel. stressed alloy panels attached to front, rear, side bulkheads and undertray

BODY PANELS
re-inforced glass-fibre, color impregnated with molded in oil-cooler ducts. secured by 'pip' pins and 'dzus' fasteners. smoke grey tinted windscreen. your choice red, white, blue or yellow colors

ELECTRICAL
12 volt coil, distributor and fuel pumps

INSTRUMENTS/INTERIOR
molded glass-fibre seats, black neoprene padded covers with press stud fittings. 11" dia. steering wheel covered with thick-grip black hide. 0-10,000 electronic tach, oil pressure and water temperature gauges.

COOLING
pressurized water radiator, header tank and engine driven pump. coolant routed to engine via chassis members. oil radiators mounted on each side of ducted body section.

SUSPENSION
front: wide-based lower wish-bones and coil/spring damper units. anti-roll bar.
rear: reversed lower wishbones, top links, twin radius rods and coil/spring damper units. anti-roll bar.
all suspension mounted on spherical bearings and fully adjustable. all suspension parts chrome plated.

BRAKES
discs 9 1/4" dia. front; 8 3/4" dia. rear. hydraulic twin master cylinders actuated by compensating mechanism. fully adjustable for front

REAR SUSPENSION

REAR CHASSIS

INTERIOR

Lolita Mk1

Althought born in Poland, car nut Henry Nehrybecki lived in Australia from the age of eleven, and after finishing school began working for a Sydney MG dealer. Five years later he found it time for a new challenge and tried his luck in the UK working as a mechanic for Eric Broadley's Lola stables, returning to Australia two years later on an epic year-long drive in a tax-free Morris 850! Arriving back in Australia in 1962 he found a job at a BMC dealer, with the added perk

of being allowed to use the dealer's service garage in his spare time. It was during the evenings and weekends that his own car took shape; the Lolita, the name of which was derived from the Lola.

Two years after his return to Australia the Lolita was finished. It was built from a steel tube spaceframe that Nehrybecki had nickel chrome welded in just four weekends. Suspension was independent all round, coming from various sources, while the magnesium wheels were designed and made by Nehrybecki. The engine, a 1071cc Cooper S shipped in from England, was mounted in the rear of the spaceframe at a forward angle of 60 degrees, while the weight distribution was 40/60. Body and cycle guards were made in aluminium by Stan Brown, headlamps were Lucas

specification

Car	**Lolita Mk1**
Wheels driven	**Rear**
Built	**Artarmon (AUS)**
Years	**1964**
Number	**1**
Featured car	**Ian Pope (AUS)**

spots, and rear lights were ordinary Mini units. All in all the Lolita looked like a true Clubman's racer, although its looks did have its disadvantages. The Lolita was placed into the open sports car class in Australia, and had to compete with much bigger machinery like the Lotus 23. It eventually raced in the under-1100cc class and became well-known in Australia's racing circles.

Sports Car World magazine tested the Lolita when new in 96bhp configuration at Oran Park circuit, writing: "The car requires an infinitely gentle touch in all facets of driving to get the best out of it. It accelerates quite brutally and power on tap in the corners is sufficient to correct oversteer tendencies almost before they happen."

Nehrybecki sold the car to Ian Pope, who had helped him build it. Pope traded it later for a Triumph TR2 only to buy the Lolita back in 1980. He restored the car and still owns it to this day, now fitted with a 1330cc Cooper S engine.

Lolita Mk2

After his experience with the first Lolita Henry Nehrybecki decided in 1967 to build a second model. By this time he had set up Lolita Automobile Developments with his mate Ian Pope. Their idea was to make it a very different car from the 1964 Lolita, by that time called the Lolita Mk1. In keeping with the Can Am fashion of the late sixties Nehrybecki designed a central fibreglass monocoque with spaceframe sections

specification

Car	**Lolita Mk2**
Wheels driven	**Rear**
Built	**Artarmon (AUS)**
Years	**1967**
Number	**1**
Featured car	**Greg Neal (AUS)**

attached both front and rear. The original plan was to fit a two-litre twin-cam engine, but money did not allow, so the builders got hold of an Cooper S unit instead; a 1310cc engine from the rally Mini of Australian race ace Bob Holden.

Like in the Lolita Mk1 the engine was canted forwards, this time by 45 degrees. The independent suspension used Lolita's own wishbones, Triumph Herald uprights at the front, and adjustable torsion bars both front and rear. Disc brakes were fitted all round. The aerodynamic

Looking nothing like its older brother, here's...

LOLITA NUMBER TWO

You'll have a hard job buying one — unless you gather a bunch of fellows around and order one each. But Lolita The Second sounds and looks like a successful race car.

Lolita Mk2

fibreglass body came in four easy-to-remove sections: front and rear plus the two doors. Big air ducts were placed in the rear section covering the engine to provide cold air to the oil cooler (right) and the Mini Cooper radiator (left), as viewed from the back. The windscreen-free Lolita Mk2 was really a single-seater, although two people could fit on the padded seat.

When finished, the car looked like a scaled-down version of the fearsome McLaren M8 Can Am racer, its original orange colour making it look even more like it (the car was later painted red with a yellow stripe, as featured). The car was tested by engine supplier Bob Holden in 1967 at Sydney's Oran Park, fitted with massive 12in tyres and an added rear wing, but the latter proved unnecessary and was removed. Holden also raced the car over the next few seasons at Warwick Farm, Calder, and Bathurst, and it soon became well-known. At the Mount Panorama circuit the car achieved a speed of 124.3mph on the Conrod Straight. Nehrybecki told *Sports Car World* in June 1969 he was willing to build more Lolita Mk2s providing he had orders for four or more, each on 50 per cent deposit. However, it never happened, and so the car remained a one-off.

The Lolita Mk2, equipped with an Alfa-Romeo DOHC 1500cc engine, was sold in the early seventies and hillclimbed throughout the decade. It was completely restored years later, the Mini Cooper S engine now replaced with a 1380cc. Its current owner continues to use the car for sprints and races.

Maya GT

The Maya GT originally began life in 1966 as the Camber GT (pages 24-25). With only a handful of cars built, the Camber GT was shown at the 1967 Racing Car Show, but instigators George Holmes and Derek Bishop only then found out that the car's headlights were positioned too low, and as such were illegal. In addition, they had made an agreement with motor accessory company Checkpoint Limited to market and distribute the car, which lead to more problems, ultimately leading to a split between the two men.

After Holmes and Bishop went their separate ways, Holmes continued with restyling the front end of the car. He renamed it the Maya GT, after his wife's horse, designing a new logo featuring a running horse, somewhat resembling that of the Ford Mustang. Holmes' initial idea was to fit rectangular headlights and position them higher than had been done previously, but only one car was built (far right) with this feature. He subsequently reverted to round lights, positioning them at a legal height by placing binnacles in the front end of the bonnet. Short bumpers were now located underneath them, while the grille had two vertical openings, instead of horizontal.

specification

Car	**Maya GT**
Wheels driven	**Front**
Built	**Camber Sands (GB)**
Years	**1967-1969**
Number	**6**
Featured car	**Kazuo Maruyama (J)**

MAYA
G·T·

The Maya's restyled front end certainly wasn't as pretty as the Camber's original nose, but at least it was road legal. The car was still based on a square tube chassis frame, using both Mini subframes, with the front-mounted engine positioned behind the radiator, and a fibreglass body reinforced with steel. There were plans to race the Maya GT more extensively, but this never got off the ground. Holmes managed to sell another six cars with help from distributors Checkpoint Limited before tragedy struck when he was killed in a sad road accident in 1968. While driving his own Maya GT, Holmes saw an injured bird in the road. He stopped and went out to rescue the little animal, but another driver had not noticed him and ran him over. Production of the Maya GT was stopped immediately after Holmes' death.

It is uncertain whether any of the six Mayas still survive in their original shape. The car pictured here is a Maya GT, but it has been fitted with the Camber front end. When first bought, its owner was given a new Maya nose to use, but evidently it was never attached. At least one more car was converted back to a Camber GT nose, while another one was destroyed in a fire. The whereabouts of the remaining three cars are unknown.

McCoy GT

The McCoy differs from the other cars in this book because it derived not only from the Mini, but firstly from another car: the Clan Crusader. The latter car had originally been designed and engineered in 1971 by a couple of ex-Lotus men, among them Brian Luff (see Status Minipower and Status 365), Paul Haussauer, John Frayling and Arthur Birchall. Birchall had run Lotus' works racing team as chief engineer and was naturally involved with the engineering of the car. The Crusader was powered by a Hillman Imp engine at the rear and built with a fibreglass monocoque body. About 350 were sold between 1971 and 1974, at which point the company was sold to a Cypriot truck manufacturer, which never ended up building any of the cars.

Ten years later Birchall found it time for a re-introduction of the car. Although the Crusader's lines still looked fresh in 1984, Birchall asked the original designer, John Frayling, to update the design, renaming it the McCoy. The square headlights were changed to round ones and the rear side screens were reduced in size, but these were the only noticeable differences on the exterior. A prototype was built using an old Crusader shell, although all the body panels were replaced; just the windscreen remained untouched. An even bigger difference, however, lay

specification

Car	**McCoy GT**
Wheels driven	**Front**
Built	**Barnham Broom (GB)**
Years	**1982-2002**
Number	**Approximately 100**
Featured car	**David White/Steven Poole (GB)**

66

underneath the restyled monocoque body. The engine and gearbox, now from a Mini, were moved to the front, and both Mini subframes, as well as a number of other Mini parts, were used. The radiator came from an Austin Metro and was placed in front of the engine to keep the bonnet line low. Brian Luff, who'd also worked on the Crusader, developed the chassis, and the McCoy was tested at Heriot-Watt University in Edinburgh – even a crash test was carried out there.

Between 1984 and 1990 Birchall Automotive sold around 85 McCoys, of which four or five were estates named McIvoy (above). Basic kit prices for a McCoy started at £1600 ex VAT. By 1990 Arthur Birchall was having health problems and he decided to end production. He sold the building and selling rights of the McCoy to one of his former employees, who built another fifteen or so cars under the NG Wynes Glassfibre Limited name, later McCoy Cars.

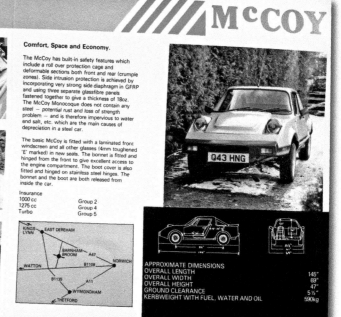

Midas Bronze

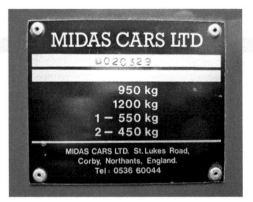

Harold Dermott bought the rights to build the Mini Marcos in July 1975, setting up D&H Fibreglass Techniques together with Maurice Holt. They soon offered a redesigned Mini Marcos, but their true ambition was to sell a new car of their own. They asked well-known kit car designer Richard Oakes to base a new car on the Marcos, but he preferred to start from scratch. By early 1978 a design was finished and work began on a prototype.

specification

Car	**Midas Bronze**
Wheels driven	**Front**
Built	**Clanfield/Corby (GB)**
Years	**1978-1988**
Number	**350**
Featured car	**Tom Berkouwer (NL)**

The car, unveiled at the Performance Car Show in London's Alexandra Palace, was named Midas – Dermott liked the name Lotus, but wanted his car to start with the letter 'M' in reference to the Mini. Both the press and the public reacted enthusiastically, but the car was not yet ready for production. Dermott himself carried out most of the testing in Europe and combined much of it with a family holiday! The press release said: "While the family played I-Spy, Harold Dermott was able to hold a highly illegal speed, hitting each apex just right, balancing the car perfectly on the throttle and gearbox – sheer bliss – and all at better than 40mpg." Arthur Birchall, manufacturer of the McCoy (pages 66-67) and ex-Team Lotus staff member, was hired to develop the suspension. The Mini's front subframe was used, while the rear was fitted with the Mini's trailing arms.

The Midas was offered for sale as a complete kit without engine and gearbox for £3250. The body shell was of exceptional quality – completely built up the car was 25 kilograms lighter than a Mini 1275 GT, but had a torsional rigidity that was 17 times greater. The windscreen was sourced from a Fiat 126, door mirrors from a Renault 14, and rear lights from a Triumph TR7.

On August 25th 1979 the first Midas was delivered. Dermott was eager to make a link with Formula One because of Arthur Birchall's involvement with the suspension. When Gordon Murray, Technical Director of racing car manufacturer Brabham, showed an interest in the car, Dermott asked him to redesign it. So, after 57 Mk1s were built the Mk2 made its appearance. Murray restyled the front and rear, making it more aerodynamic (it was tested in the Brabham wind tunnel), and a new moulded dashboard was added to the car. Although the car had always just been named 'Midas,' it was later referred to as the Midas Bronze after the new Metro-based Midas Gold made its appearance in 1985. Once again Dermott had thought up some catchy words to praise the car: "An imaginative concept for imaginative people. You can get something like it from Stuttgart, or Maranello, or even Newport Pagnell. But the best concepts come from Corby."

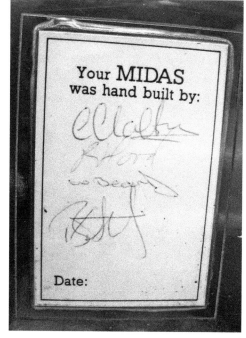

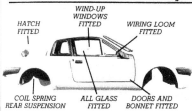

Mini Jem Mk1

After DART-instigator Desmond 'Dizzy' Addicott became fed up with the project to build a Mini GT in 1965 (see DART), he sold his plans to racing enthusiast Jeremy Delmar-Morgan for £750. It took Delmar-Morgan a year to come up with a production version of the car, naming it the Mini Jem. The first Mini Jems were finished in the summer of 1966, but the car was officially launched at the Racing Car Show in January 1967. The Mini Jem differed in styling from the original DART prototype, but was still easily recognizable from its aerodynamic shape. Delmar-Morgan had used his nickname, Jem, to name the car, but it is often believed he used it to tease Jem Marsh. Marsh of Marcos Cars had been involved in the DART project, too, but after an argument with Desmond Addicott had decided to split and work on a similar car of his own; that became the Mini Marcos.

specification

Car	**Mini Jem Mk1**
Wheels driven	**Front**
Built	**London/High Wycombe (GB)**
Years	**1966-1969**
Number	**About 35**
Featured car	**Ivor Miller (IRL)**

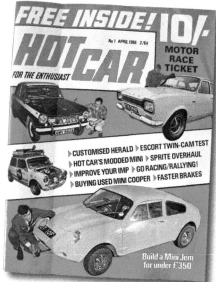

Like the Mini Marcos, the Mini Jem was available as a monocoque body shell. It was offered for sale at just £189 – ten pounds less than the very cheap Mini Marcos. Delmar-Morgan built and sold over twenty shells from his workshop in west London, although he also sold a few cars completely finished at around £500 each.

However, most buyers decided to save money and build it themselves.

The Mini Jem used Mini running gear and subframes, but the finish was rather crude. *Hot Car* magazine asked BEA pilot Edward Dunn to build one, and enthusiastically wrote that a buyer could build one in under a week, at a limited budget of less than £350. Delmar-Morgan raced

a Mini Jem himself, coming second in class in the Nürburgring 500 kilometer race in 1966. By November of that year he had moved production to Penn Garage in High Wycombe, whose owner, Robin Statham, rented him some space. Delmar-Morgan saw it as a temporary solution, with plans to move to new premises close to Silverstone, but this was never realised. He delivered another twelve body shells from Penn Garage, but by that time had had enough of it.

Delmar-Morgan sold the Mini Jem project to Robin Statham in 1967.

Mini Jem Mk2/Mk3

When Robin Statham took over production of the Mini Jem from Jeremy Delmar-Morgan in 1967, the car wasn't exactly known as the most sophisticated. The body shells built by Delmar-Morgan were pretty crude, and buyers needed some skills to produce proper cars from them. Statham decided to address this problem by offering an improved kit. He began modifying the car, which resulted in the Mini Jem Mk2. It was officially launched by his company, Fellpoint Limited, at the 1969 Racing Car Show in London.

The new Mini Jem not only had a better finish, but it was completely redesigned, too. It now sported a more raked windscreen, which had been moved back no less than nine inches. The roof line was raised to gain some headroom and so was the rear fastback line, as Statham believed it had always been raked too dramatically. No external door handles were fitted, meaning doors

had to be opened by sliding down a side screen first. The Mini Jem Mk2 was offered for sale as a kit for £350, with doors and windows fitted, painted and trimmed. Like Delmar-Morgan, Statham raced his own cars, too. His lightweight works racer was fitted with a 1293cc Cooper S engine, giving the aerodynamically-shaped car a top speed of 130mph. Sales were doing well, but Fellpoint Limited came into trouble when they tried to launch an

specification

Car	**Mini Jem Mk2/Mk3**
Wheels driven	**Front**
Built	**High Wycombe/Cricklade/Wombwell (GB)**
Years	**1968-1972/1972-1974**
Number	**Approximately 200/unknown**
Featured car	**Aurélien Bini (F)**

Mini Jem MkII

1. Shell complete in pigmented reinforced glass fibre, filled, rubbed down and sprayed with Lesonal P62, a specially developed filler primer for fibre glass bodies.
2. Front-mounted crossflow radiator and header tank supplied.
3. Power bulge moulded into bonnet to make room for extra large carburettors.
4. Dashboard left blank for any instrument arrangement.
5. Jig drilled ready to accept front and rear sub-frames.
6. Body chassis unit which will accept either hydrolastic or dry suspension.
7. Will accept side-draught Weber carburettor.
8. Aerodynamic wind-spoiler moulded in for maximum stability.
9. Accepts only Mini van petrol tank.
10. Proven on road and track over the last six years.
11. Laminated windscreen as standard.
12. Left-hand drive is available for a small extra charge.
13. Light-weight racing shell with roll-over bar available to order. Not suitable for road use.

The Mk II Mini Jem comes complete with the many extras quoted below included in the list price:
Shell finished in pigmented reinforced glass fibre, filled, rubbed down and sprayed in the undercoat. Doors, bonnet, windscreen, rear screen and side screens fitted.
Draught excluder, door catches, door pulls, door stays, hinges, all fitted.
Interior trim fitted, i.e. carpets, roof lining, door panel, rear panels and dash panel.
Radiator, header tank and badges supplied.
Body/Chassis units supplied only by the manufacturers, Jem Cars.

DIMENSIONS	
Weight:	complete car approx. 11 cwt
Weight:	basic shell 350 lb
Length overall:	11 ft 3 ins
Width overall:	4 ft 9 ins
Height overall:	3 ft 6 ins
Seat base to roof:	34 ins
Width at shoulder height:	46 ins
Seat back to pedals (maximum):	44 ins
Luggage space:	10½ cu.ft

extraordinary new car called the Futura. Based on a brand new Volkswagen Beetle chassis, the Futura came with a big and very steeply raked windscreen that hinged on a tube frame, allowing the driver and passenger entry to the car. The Futura's design came from Statham and interest was huge. The trouble was the prototype, which had been so costly that it brought an end to Fellpoint Limited, taking the division Jem Cars with it. In July 1971 both companies went into liquidation, by which time Statham had built around 160 Mini Jems. The rights to producing the car were taken over by High Performance Mouldings of Cricklade in Wiltshire, and in 1972 the Jem was once again back in production. In the summer of that year the Mini Jem Mk3 was launched, now available with an opening rear hatch. In early 1974 the moulds changed hands again, but by now production had almost stopped. Fellpoint built one Mini Jem Estate (pages 124-125), based on an early Mk2 car. It was probably a prototype that never made production.

THE JEM Mk II *IN ACTION*

114

FOR FURTHER DETAILS SEND S.A.E. & 1/6d. P.O. TO
FELLPOINT LTD., PENN GARAGE, HAZLEMERE ROAD, PENN, BUCKS

Mini Marcos GT Mk1/Mk2/Mk3

Marcos boss Jem Marsh had been involved with the DART (pages 30-31) after Desmond 'Dizzy' Addicott had asked his fibreglass department, Falcon Shells, to make a mould from the steel prototype and produce body shells from it. Addicott was unhappy with the result, leading to a split between the two men. Jem Marsh set off to create a Mini GT of his own, and this became the first Mini Marcos. Brian Moulton, who worked for Marsh, did the redesign of the car and based it on one of the DART body shells rejected

by Addicott, but changed it rather drastically, focusing even more on the sporty ambitions that Marsh had with the car. The finished product was an easy to fabricate fibreglass monocoque with running gear & subframes from a Mini. One of

specification

Car	**Mini Marcos GT Mk1/Mk2/Mk3**
Wheels driven	**Front**
Built	**Bradford-on-Avon (GB)**
Years	**1965-1966/1966-1967/1967-1970**
Number	**143/unknown/665**
Featured car	**Turtle Trading Ltd (J)**

the first cars finished was prepared for racing by Janspeed and made its debut at the Castle Combe circuit in September 1965 where it did surprisingly well.

The official launch was held at the Racing Car Show in January 1966, and by that time the Mini Marcos was offered for sale at a very low £199 for a basic shell. According to the advertisements a customer could build it up as a car in 15 to 20 hours. One of these customers was the professional deep sea diver Jean-Claude Hrubon from Paris. He built a car with a 1287cc Cooper S engine and raced it at Montlhéry, where he was asked to have his car driven in the Le Mans 24 hours Race of June 1966; the drivers were Jean-Louis Marnat and Claude Ballot-Lena. Jem Marsh also went to Le Mans that year, although he was not particularly pleased: "I had nothing to do with the preparation of the car and was horrified when I saw it. I didn't think it would last a lap." In fact, it came home fifteenth overall and was the first British car to finish the race. Marsh entered an aerodynamically-altered works car (above, right) for the 24 hours race the following year, and clocked it at 141mph on the Mulsanne Straight. Unfortunately, it did not finish because of a broken timing gear. However, by then the Mini Marcos was selling well and a Mk2 version was now available. This car had a different floor, slightly altered wheelarches and front end, plus slide-up windows in aluminium frames instead of fixed Perspex windows with sliding ventilators. A very similar Mk3 version was introduced in 1971, available with an opening rear hatch. As well as England, the Mini Marcos was also produced under licence in Ireland and South Africa.

Mini Marcos GT Mk4/Mk5/Mk6

By 1970 Marcos Cars Components Limited had managed to sell hundreds of the Mini Marcos, but trouble lay ahead. The company had just launched the four-seater Mantis, but the ungainly-styled car was not much of a success. There had also been high costs involved in exploring the American market – to no avail, plus the move to a new factory. All in all it lead to the downfall of the company in 1971, but Jem Marsh did not give up. After selling the company to

Rob Walker (see MiniSprint), who renamed the company Marcos Limited, Marsh established himself at a small factory in Newbury from where he started working for Walker on the Mini Marcos Mk4 (pictured); it was introduced in the summer of 1972. The car was four inches longer and slightly higher than its predecessors, allowing space for a small rear seat. It had a new floor that was based on that of the Mini Traveller, and came with an opening rear hatch as standard, giving much better access to the rear platform of the car. After three years the company changed hands again when it was taken over by Harold Dermott's D&H Fibreglass Techniques Limited in Oldham. The car changed very little during this time, and Dermott offered it for sale up until 1981. By then his company had

specification

Car	**Mini Marcos GT Mk4/Mk5/Mk6**
Wheels driven	**Front**
Built	**Westbury/Oldham/Semington (GB)**
Years	**1972-1981/1991-1995/2005-present**
Number	**626/64/unknown**
Featured cars	**Richard Porter (GB); Bill Whithey (GB)**

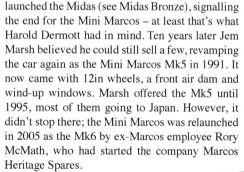

launched the Midas (see Midas Bronze), signalling the end for the Mini Marcos – at least that's what Harold Dermott had in mind. Ten years later Jem Marsh believed he could still sell a few, revamping the car again as the Mini Marcos Mk5 in 1991. It now came with 12in wheels, a front air dam and wind-up windows. Marsh offered the Mk5 until 1995, most of them going to Japan. However, it didn't stop there; the Mini Marcos was relaunched in 2005 as the Mk6 by ex-Marcos employee Rory McMath, who had started the company Marcos Heritage Spares.

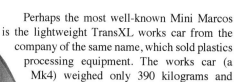

Perhaps the most well-known Mini Marcos is the lightweight TransXL works car from the company of the same name, which sold plastics processing equipment. The works car (a Mk4) weighed only 390 kilograms and was tested extensively at the Rolls-Royce premises in Crewe; the same place the conrods were made. Fitted with a 1480cc engine it was raced by Steven Roberts from 1977 onwards. Out of 98 races Roberts won 36 times and had 74 podium placings. He won the Modsport Championship twice and also set four land speed records that stand to this day. After 1979 the car became an exhibit: first in the London Science museum, and then in the Beaulieu Motor Museum until 1984.

Mini Minus

During the late sixties Lotus Cars of Norfolk expanded rapidly, although unfortunately not to the liking of all the workforce. In 1969 a group of employees resigned to start up on their own. They were mysteriously known as the 'Group of 69,' and together came up with various projects. Two of the men were Brian Luff (see Status Minipower and Status 365) and Keith Lain. After Luff designed the Mini Minus, Lain started Minus Cars in the early eighties, working from a converted farm workshop in Wymondham, Norfolk. Initially, the car was offered as the Status Mini Minus, but as Luff moved to Jersey, he gave the job to Lain and the car was renamed.

specification

Car	**Minus**
Wheels driven	**Front**
Built	**Wymondham (GB)**
Years	**1982-2008**
Number	**Unknown**
Featured car	**Terry Handley (GB)**

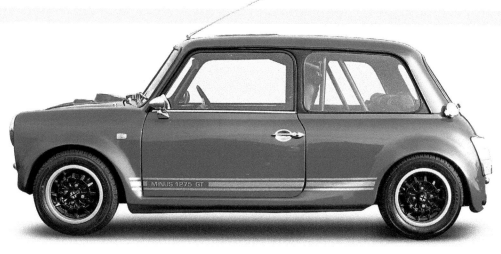

The idea behind the car was simple; to offer a replacement body for the Mini that would never rust. The fibreglass body shells that Lain fabricated all used Mini parts, including the doors, which had to be lowered at the bottom to allow for the fact that the car was now six inches lower, since the body of the original Mini had been sectioned. As all the sectioning came from the waist of the car the glass components remained untouched, allowing customers buying a body shell to still fit the original glass from their donor Mini. Steel frames were fitted around the door apertures of the fibreglass body to provide more strength, and to allow mounting of the seatbelts, and a steel rollover bar incorporated into a solid basic framework. The only changes required during construction were lowering of the radiator and the addition of some earth returns to the wiring loom.

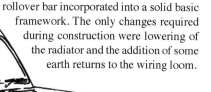

Initial prices for the Mini Minus started at £525 plus VAT, but rose to £850 plus VAT in the mid-eighties. Some extras were available, of which modified doors (at £65 a pair) and primer body finish (£160) were the most opted for.

In the mid-eighties Keith Lain came up with some more variations on the Mini Minus. One of them was a Minus Maxi that was a rather square Mini Clubman-style estate with off-road styling influences and a hatchback. Another was the Minus 4R2 that came with a tube spaceframe and rear-mounted engine. It was named after the Austin Metro 6R4 rallycar, which had 6 cylinders, a rear-mounted engine, and 4-wheel-drive.

In 2001 Lain sold the Minus rights to Shaun Dyson, who offered body shells from £2250 soon after the takeover.

MiniSprint

The idea of the MiniSprint came as early as 1964 when Neville Trickett met Geoff Thomas, who raced a Mini Cooper S and ran a car accessory business in Dorset. They came up with the idea to cut a Mini through both the windscreen pillars and the waistline. The result was an aerodynamically-improved car with reduced frontal area. Trickett began working on the first car in October 1965, after which Thomas financed a workshop in Willisdown, Bournemouth. Trickett removed 1½ inches from the body above and below the waistline, and another 1½ inches from the pillars. He increased the rake of the front screen as well as the rear, and gas-welded everything back together, removing all the seams, too. The windscreens had to be made especially for the car (although 25 per cent reputedly broke

during fitting), while side and rear screens were made of Perspex. The cut-down job also resulted in the fitting of a new bonnet and fibreglass boot lid, as well as lowering of the seat frames.

Immediately after the unveiling of the MiniSprint, demand for it rose for both racing and road use. One customer was race ace Rob Walker,

specification

Car	**MiniSprint**
Wheels driven	**Front**
Built	**Wallisdown/Corsley (GB)**
Years	**1965-1967**
Number	**Approximately 100**
Featured cars	**Kazuo Maruyama (J), Paul Wiggington (GB)**

who ordered no fewer then fifty cars to sell through his garage business, meaning Trickett and his small team had to work hard to get them all finished on time. The workshop later moved, initially ending up at Walker's Corsley Garage close to Warminster. Walker became the distributor for the MiniSprint and quite a few cars went abroad. In just one year Trickett built around 85 MiniSprints. His later MiniSprints were lowered by 4 inches instead of 3, although the best-known MiniSprint – the black lightweight racer shown on these pages – was even lower. At 42 inches in height overall it was an incredible 11 inches lower than a standard Mini, and was fitted with a very clever wishbone rear suspension mounted on a special subframe, adapted from the Mini's front suspension. Doors were made of asbestos, and the bonnet and boot lid from fibreglass.

In late 1966 the production rights for the MiniSprint were sold to BMC dealers Stewart and Ardern, but it is believed no more than a dozen were built before the project was sold on. By this time numerous privateers had started building 'chopped' Minis of their own, of which a good example is the blue car shown here. Neville Trickett has recently started building MiniSprints again; this time from his home in France.

WALKER-GTR

Nimbus Coupé

I f the Cox GTM and Unipower GT were the 'Mini-Miuras' of the sixties, then the Davrian Mk8 and the Nimbus Coupé were their equivalents of the eighties. The latter is without doubt the least well known, although it had a lot to offer when launched in 1984.

The Nimbus Coupé was the brainchild of Ian Shearer who dreamt it up while living in East Sussex, but only once he had moved to Whitchurch, Hampshire did production begin. Shearer teamed up with Ian McLean who financed the new company Nimbus Projects Limited. Boat builders Custom Moulds, in Andover (above, right), was sub-contracted to build the bodies for the car. The body shell was a fibreglass monocoque with kevlar reinforcement and balsa sandwich bulkheads, sills and pillars. Front suspension and disc brakes were partly Vauxhall Viva, partly Mini, while the windscreen was sourced from the Ford Escort Mk2. Other

specification

Car	**Nimbus Coupé**
Wheels driven	**Rear**
Built	**Whitchurch (GB)**
Years	**1984-1987**
Number	**24**
Featured car	**Simon Harbot (GB)**

Nimbus Coupé

ANALYSIS:NIMBUS

non-Mini parts used for the Nimbus were Reliant door hinges, Morris Marina door handles, Volkswagen Scirocco head lamps, and an Austin Allegro or Alfasud radiator. The works prototype was fitted with a tuned 1400cc Mini engine and, according to *Kit Car* magazine, could reach 120mph at 6500 revs in top gear. The downside with the Nimbus Coupé was that buyers needed some serious skills to build one. The basic kit cost £1485 and was supplied with dashboard, centre tunnel and inner sills fitted and bonded, and the body finished in etch primer. The doors, rear hatch, bonnet and engine cover were supplied loose.

In early 1986 Nimbus Projects Limited went into liquidation, reputedly due to Shearer's bad management. Anthony Coleman, one of the workforce at Custom Moulds, decided to take over production of the Nimbus Coupé, together with Ian McLean. Unfortunately, McLean died soon after their decision to give the car a new lease of life. Coleman decided to carry on with the project, and even planned to develop an open-top version, which was to be called McLean – as a tribute to its financial backer. However, demand for the Nimbus Coupé proved minimal, and in 1987 Coleman ended work on the project.

According to John Stone, who built the body shells for Custom Moulds, 24 bodies were finished in total, some of which were used in motor sport – Swindon garage owner Niall Johanson competed in the National Rally Championship in a 1450cc Mini-engined Nimbus Coupé, while Garry Shillabeer, from Devon, also raced one.

Nimbus Don Parker Special

Although this all-English car has its Mini Cooper-engine mounted at the rear, driving its rear wheels, it actually is a prototype for a South African sports car that came with a front-mounted Ford-engine! Its chequered history began back in the mid-fifties, when South Africans Bob van Niekirk and Willie Meisner formed the Glassport Motor Company in Springbok. When the two motoring men went to the United Kingdom to learn more about building fibreglass body shells, it was decided to have a body built in England. Former Rootes-stylist Verster de Witt had designed a body to fit a ladder frame that was to be equipped with a Ford Popular-engine. When it was finished in April 1957, moulds were taken from the body and shipped back to South Africa.

There the production of the GSM Delta was to follow soon. Meanwhile, a Riley-engined racing version was built by former sculptor, painter, stonemason, welder and panel beater Don Parker, who was also a great racing enthusiast. Parker brought the Special with him when he moved to the UK in 1957. When he saw a special that used Mini Cooper mechanicals in the mid-1960s there, he was inspired to do the same. He bought a Cooper S-engine direct from the BMC Works department in 1965, and changed his Nimbus so radically that it now was rear-engined. Mini Cooper disc brakes were fitted too, as was a Shorrocks supercharger turning the lightweight racer into a

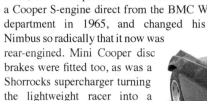

specification

Car	**Nimbus DP Special**
Wheels driven	**Rear**
Built	**West Malling (GB)**
Years	**1957/1965**
Number	**1**
Featured car	**Bryan Purves (GB)**

Nimbus Don Parker Special

seriously fast machine. He and his brother-in-law, Mike Hentall, sprinted and hillclimbed the special for some years. Hentall later took it over and carried on using the car for motor sports. He fitted a truck-sourced supercharger with a vastly increased capacity, and now producing about 155bhp at a weight of approximately 450kg. Hentall: "Even running on pure methanol we were going through pistons every other meeting, but when we could hold her together we collected our share of awards at Prescott and Shelsley in the 'Golden Oldies' Class." Eventually Hentall took the car to Portugal in 1988 before selling it. In 2000, the Nimbus special was brought back to the UK, and it was sympathetically restored in 2002 to its former glory, although without the supercharger. It has recently been repainted baby blue and red.

Nimrod

As an illustrator for a Chichester newspaper, Mike Jupp (pictured, right) was most surprised when, in 1969, he was asked to design a car. It had to be based on Mini mechanics and be a fun, beach buggy-style car. Jupp liked the concept of what he now calls a 'Juppmobile' and began drawing. Intrigued by World War II machinery, he was influenced by both the Volkswagen Kübelwagen and Schwimmwagen, so perhaps it is not surprising that the Nimrod he designed had some amphibious characteristics, although the Nimrod name derived from the famous Nimrod fighter planes. A local company was sub-contracted to weld the chassis, while

nimrod

FIRST CLASS   FIRST CLASS   ADMIT TWO

ADMIT TWO   FIRST CLASS   FIRST CLASS

WPJ 596G

AN EXCITING
NEW-LOOK FOR YOUR MINI
THIS 2 SEAT MINI-BASED KIT— JUST THE TICKET!

Your NIMROD kit consists of:—

Space frame chassis—fully rust-proofed and painted.
GRP body panels.
Laminated windscreen.
Laminated rear screen.
Roll over bar.
1 pair of seats and subframes (selection of seats available).
1 pair of 3-point harness seat belts.
1 pair of rectangular headlights.
1 pair of combination rear lights (side, tail, indicator, fog, reverse).
1 pair of rear shock absorbers.
New fuel tank.
Battery box, earth and main live feed cable.

All above items are factory fitted to ensure a perfect fit, professional finish, and simplicity of construction.

Optional extras available are:—

Set of 5 × 10 alloy wheels (recommended).
Set of 165 × 10 tyres (recommended).
Tonneau cover.

EVERYTHING ELSE IS SUPPLIED IN THE BASE PRICE

T.A.C.C.O. 24 Tything Way, Wincanton, Somerset. BA9 9EU
Telephone: Wincanton (0963) 33873 (24 hours)

WPJ 596G

specification

Car	Nimrod
Wheels driven	Front
Built	Hunston/Wincanton (GB)
Years	1973-1974/1979-1986
Number	5/approximately 10
Featured car	Mike Jupp (GB)

fibreglass specialist and carpenter Ray Jay of Hunston was asked to build the car Jupp had drawn. Jay started working on a prototype from his parents' farmhouse, but was only halfway through when the people who initially proposed the idea for the Nimrod withdrew from the project, leaving Jupp and Ray with nothing but a half-finished car. They decided to put it on the road themselves, and Jupp paid Jay to complete the first Nimrod, which was finished in 1972. The ladder frame chassis came with a plywood floor while the rollbar was made from a scaffold tube. The fibreglass body was an open two-seater with very high sills and no doors. Running between the windscreen and the rear screen was a bar to give the body a bit more strength, with a black vinyl roof attached. A Hillman Hunter provided the headlights and rear lights, and the petrol tank came from a Mini Van.

Jupp admits that he wanted to give the car as much of a 'beach buggy-look' as he possibly could, and designed chunky rear mudflaps to give the impression of wide tyres! Jupp took delivery of the car and used it well. He even drove the car on a holiday to Transylvania in 1974 with a trailer behind it to carry a tent and other gear. When a friend of Jupp's asked for a second car, Jay began to think about limited production, eventually building another four Nimrods. In 1979 the car

was offered by a company called Nova, but it is unknown whether any cars were ever sold. A few cars were built by Nigel Talbott and his company TACCO in Wincanton two years later, but it is believed no more than fifteen Nimrods were built in total. By 1986 the car had stopped being produced.

87

Nota Fang

Guy Buckingham was a clockmaker in Buckinghamshire who became an engineer for the RAF in the Second World War. He moved to Australia in 1952 where he decided to set up Nota Cars. 'Nota' is said to stand for 'No other transport available,' 'Not a special,' and also a variation on 'motorcar,' pronounced 'notacar' by Buckingham's then baby son, Chris.

Once Buckingham had settled in Parramatta, just outside Sydney, he was soon building various racing and hillclimbing specials, mostly one-offs. One of these was rear-powered by a Mini engine as early as 1963. By 1968 he had built a car based on a Morris Cooper S that had been crashed and left sitting in the workshop. Guy's son Chris designed the car, called the Nota Type 4, although it was soon renamed Nota Fang to compliment its sharp appearance! The Buckinghams decided to offer the Nota Fang model for sale from AU $1999. Based on a steel tube spaceframe with sheet steel undertray the Fang could be fitted with any Mini engine, ranging from a basic 850cc to a specially-developed 80bhp-strong 1293cc. Equipped with the latter the car was capable of 115mph, achieving 0-50mph in just over 6 seconds and the standing 400 metres

specification

Car	**Nota Fang**
Wheels driven	**Rear**
Built	**Parramatta (AUS), Fairford (GB), Dural (AUS)**
Years	**1968-1975**
Number	**107 (including non-Mini-powered)**
Featured car	**Nola & John Seymour (AUS)**

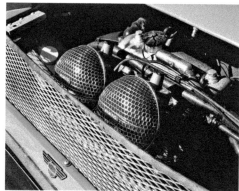

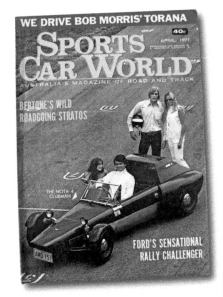

in less than 17 seconds. Rear suspension was of Mini origin, with locked steering. Hillman Imp swing axles with coil springs and Koni telescopic dampers were fitted to another Mini subframe at the front of the car. The steering rack and drum brakes were also sourced from the Imp. Bodies were made of fibreglass, except for the side panels, which were aluminium. Unlike the rear wheels, the wheels at the front were shielded by separate cycle guards; a bit like a miniature Allard J2.

The Nota Fang was a success and the Buckinghams built 64 examples before Guy returned to England in the early seventies. Chris stayed in Australia. Guy introduced the Nota Fang in the UK in 1972 and built a few more before he retired. Under Chris' management Nota Engineering is still active today, with a modern version of the Fang still available. However, the current model is no longer Mini-powered, engines now varying from Honda two-litre V-tecs to Toyota 1800s.

Ogle SX1000

In December 1961 David Ogle, of the design house with the same name, presented his first Ogle SX1000, and it soon caused a stir in the motor industry. Here was a car that used all of the Mini's mechanicals – complete floorpan, inner wings and part of the bulkhead, engine and gearbox, plus subframes, steering and suspension – but changed completely thanks to a new fibreglass body shell.

From 1962 onwards David Ogle Limited transformed any Mini into its baby GT at its Letchworth factory, and thanks to the design and excellent finish it was not hard to find customers for the SX1000, priced at £550. It was later revealed, by Ogle's then-chairman John Ogier, it cost considerably more to build the car: "It would have been cheaper to give any customer £300 and told him to go away!" However, at BMC – which had initially refused to supply new parts – the apparent success of David Ogle Limited did not go unnoticed. BMC eventually agreed to supply new parts, but insisted that no mention of the word 'Mini' was used in promotional material. From then on Ogle supplied

specification

Car	**Ogle SX1000**
Wheels driven	**Front**
Built	**Letchworth (GB)**
Years	**1962-1964**
Number	**69**
Featured car	**Geoffrey Hunter (GB)**

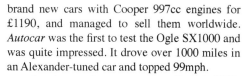

brand new cars with Cooper 997cc engines for £1190, and managed to sell them worldwide. *Autocar* was the first to test the Ogle SX1000 and was quite impressed. It drove over 1000 miles in an Alexander-tuned car and topped 99mph.

A racing version was announced later in 1962, called the Ogle Lightweight GT. It had a lighter body, built-in rollbar, lowered suspension, stripped interior with bucket seats, and came in a special maroon and biscuit colour scheme. It is often said that Ogle's then-director, Sir John Whitmore – who later became European Saloon Car Champion driving a Lotus Cortina – raced it, but he himself is adamant he never did. However, it was David Ogle who drove the Ogle Lightweight GT on his way to Brands Hatch in May 1962 when he was killed in a road accident. Close to Welwyn, Hertfordshire, Ogle crashed into a lorry and was killed instantly. The company was subsequently taken over by SX1000 designer Tom Karen, who had come from Ford's design department, having to prove he was able to run Ogle's in six months. He did, and became general manager and chief designer for another 37 years before retiring. After David Ogle's death, Karen decided to cease production of the SX1000 and the last cars were built in late 1963, bringing the total, including the pre-production cars, to 69. The moulds were sold to boat-builder Norman Fletcher in 1966 (see Fletcher GT).

HMM. WILL OUR CHIMNEY BE WIDE ENOUGH?

Peel Viking Sport GT

The Isle of Man isn't exactly renowned for its car industry, but Cyril Cannel from Peel, on the island's west coast, made a brave attempt to put the 'Man' on the motoring map. An ex-RAF pilot, who had flown Hurricanes and Wellington Bombers in the Second World War, Cannel had been experimenting with fibreglass at his parents' shipyard. The idea of building cars emerged from the shortage of private cars after the war, and in combination with the attractive tax rates on the island, Cannel got enthusiastic. He formed Peel Engineering Limited in the fifties, and the first vehicle appeared in 1955: the Manxman three-wheeler

with a 250cc two-stroke engine. The Peel P50 and Peel Trident followed in the early sixties and were slightly more successful, but Peel Engineering got upscale. At the London Racing Car Show in 1966 the company introduced a four-wheeled sports car based on Mini mechanicals. It was the Peel Viking Sport GT, which used more Mini parts than any other derivative described in this book. Not only did the engine, wheels and suspension come from the Mini, but also the front bumper, head and rear lights, windscreen, rear screen, front side screens, and near enough the complete interior, including the rear seat. The doors looked very

specification

Car	**Peel Viking Sport GT**
Wheels driven	**Front**
Built	**Peel (GBM)**
Years	**1966-1967**
Number	**24**
Featured car	**Neil Hanson (GBM)**

similar to those on the Mini, but in fact were slightly cut-down fibreglass versions. The price for a body initially was £230; a little more than that of a Mini Marcos, introduced just months earlier. Like the Marcos, Cannel had to cope with the relatively high-placed engine and side-mounted radiator, both of which made it difficult to keep the bonnet line low. Comment was given from the motoring press on the rather bulbous lines of the car. The rear, however, was cleverly shaped with a Kamm tail. Luggage was accessed from the inside of the car as there was no boot lid or hatchback door.

It is believed that Peel Engineering only built a few Viking Sport GTs, although approximately twenty more cars were built after Bill Last, of Viking Performance in Suffolk, took over the company. At least five bodies were sold to The Netherlands, where Ben Konst of Wassenaar assembled the cars for Dutch customers. In the summer of 1967 Konst even won a Concours d'Elegance in one of these cars. Cyril Cannel stopped building cars after the Viking Sports GT adventure. He still lives at the Peel shipyard (pictured, left), and is currently working on a design for a Manx monorail.

Pellandini

Peter Pellandine had already made a name for himself in the early days of the specialist sports cars scene. He worked as a stylist for London coachbuilder H J Mulliner, but started on his own in 1955 with Ashley Laminates, later forming Falcon Shells. In his Waltham Abbey-based business, Pellandine produced and sold fibreglass bodies, mostly used for Ford Popular and Morris 8 underpinnings. He sold the company in 1961, although it went under three years later. Nothing more was heard of Peter Pellandine until the early seventies, when he turned up on the other side of the world in Australia to unveil his Pellandini Sports Coupé. It was a striking car with gullwing doors, which Pellandine later said had been inspired by Ferrari's infamous Dino. The Pellandini had a monocoque fibreglass chassis body structure, about which the brochure said: "It has been possible to stress the main sections of the body, floor, centre tunnel, door sills, interior wheelarches, seats, spare wheel compartment, fascia panel and even the glove box." Steel sheets

specification

Car	**Pellandini**
Wheels driven	**Rear**
Built	**Cherry Gardens (AUS)**
Years	**1971-1976**
Number	**8 (7 Coupés, 1 roadster)**
Featured car	**Max Kinsmore (AUS)**

were bonded into the fibreglass structure to strengthen the suspension points. Mini uprights were used at the front, while the rear was fitted with special aluminium ones. Both front and rear were fitted with wishbones, coil springs and telescopic dampers. *Sports Car World*, which tested the car, found it very low: "Armco at

A gutsy engine and ultra light weight make this imaginative coupe a...

PINT SIZED POWERHOUSE

Who said you couldn't get snappy performance, eye boggling looks, first class handling in an under $3000 car. BARRY CATFORD says you can.

GET A SOUTH AUSTRALIAN enthusiast talking and the chances are he'll start spouting about how Adelaide is the home of specialist sports and racing cars.

He'll rattle off names like Elfin, Asp, Birrana and maybe a few more that you haven't heard of and he'll take a lot of talking down.

And the advent of the Pellandini coupe isn't going to make the job any easier for you.

The Pellandini coupe is a Mini-based mid-engined sporty, with snappy good looks, sporty performance and a very down to earth price. And it's all South Australian.

The car's creator, Peter Pellandini, sells the cars ex-works, fully trimmed and painted for $1895 and to that you add the price of wrecked Mini (from $50 to Clubman GT depending on how fast you want to go).

So for around three grand you should be able to build up a real little stormer which will stand out in a crowd. Using Cooper S components it should go about as hard as a Nota Fang which means standing quarters in the late 14s and a 120 mph top speed.

The engine/transmission unit fits transversely just

SPORTS CAR WORLD, October, 1973 11

An announcement all too rare...

NEW AUSSIE SPORTY!

Peter Pellandine's latest Cooper-powered buzz-bomb looks pretty high priced at $4200, but it's still the cheapest open sports car you can buy on the Australian market. BARRY CATFORD drives it.

Peter Pellandine suitably attired for a winter trip in his open car. Power is Cooper S engine/transaxle in the rear, wheels are Globe magic.

Pellandini offers little protection from the wind, but excellent roll-over protection. Seats are sumptuous — each car is tailored to its buyer.

shoulder height and the feeling of having to look way up to see the top of a truck wheel, took some getting used to, but the handling was marvellous and body roll just wasn't there." Pedals were placed to fit the buyer's requirements, while the moulded seats were trimmed with leather or sheepskin and came with four-point harnesses. Windscreen and side screens were Perspex, and the pop-up headlights were operated manually by means of a lever on the fascia panel. Pellandine offered the Pellandini for sale painted and trimmed, but minus Mini mechanicals, for $1855. A fully built car with a brand new 1100cc engine was also available, as was a complete kit. The latter turned out to be the most successful; Pellandine sold seven kits and none of the ready-built cars. These figures must have been disappointing to its creator, who decided to market a new version: the Pellandini Roadster. Apart from being roofless, this model was virtually the same, but equipped with conventional side-hinged doors. A rollover bar was fitted behind the seats, and there was only an ultra low Perspex windscreen to protect the driver and passenger from the elements. Unfortunately, the Roadster didn't generate the interest Pellandine hoped

for, and only the prototype was built. Pellandine returned to the UK in 1978 where he designed and built the Volkswagen-based Pelland Sports, which was slightly more successful than the Pellandini. Pellandine later returned to Australia, and began building steam-powered cars, which he works on to this day.

Sabre Sprint

Sabre Cars was formed in 1984 in the Newcastle suburb of Wallsend by a company that made anything from sun beds to canoes, as long as it was fibreglass. Its owner, Steven Crabtree, had previously been making fibreglass panels for other kit car manufacturers, and found it time to build his own car. He designed and engineered the Sabre, which was offered from 1984 to 1986. It was a boxy car, in which the lines of the Ford Escort Mk3 are often recognised. The Sabre's body was a fibreglass monocoque reinforced with kevlar and carbon fibre to unstress the fixed points. It used the Mini's engine in its original subframe at the front, while the rear subframe was replaced by a galvanized crossmember, which carried the Mini's original suspension swinging arms, together with 12in wheel hubs and drum brakes. The car had four seats, of which the rear ones could be tilted forward to get access to the boot.

specification

Car	**Sabre Sprint**
Wheels driven	**Front**
Built	**Wallsend (GB)**
Years	**1984-1986**
Number	**Approximately 110**
Featured car	**Richard Finlay**

Sabre Sprint

Initially, the car was offered with square headlights and a glass tailgate that could be opened, but only a year after its introduction the Mk2 version was launched. By now the front had been redesigned, now sporting twin round headlights and a different radiator grille, while the rear now came with a full hatchback that opened at bumper level.

Hybrids of the two Sabre versions were also built, as can be seen by the featured car. It has the new-style front end, but the opening glass tailgate. During the redesign of the Sprint's rear, the idea of another version was born, and together with its restyled Sprint, Sabre Cars introduced the Sabre Vario (pictured, right) in 1985. It was a variation on the Sprint, but now with removable fibreglass rear roof section. Both A- and B-pillars remained, but overall it was very much like a convertible. The boot was supplied with a removable lid, which could be replaced with a hatchback estate roof. The Vario may have seemed like a good idea, but no more than a handful were sold. There was also a Sabre Camper, too, but that remained a one-off.

Although initially commended for its modern shape, the Sabre Sprint vanished after 1986, at which point about 110 cars had been built. Some of them made it into the sports scene, featuring in hillclimbing and rallying events. The Sabre's moulds initially ended up in nearby Newcastle-upon-Tyne, where FRA Mini built a replica of the standard Mini based on the monocoque undertray of the Sabre Sprint, complete with a fibreglass body shell. It's no coincidence then that FRA Minis have a Sabre floorpan shortened by 11cm.

97

Sarcon Scarab

Allan Staniforth had wanted to develop and build a sports car with a fibreglass body since 1964, but when he and his business partner, Richard Blackmore, found out that developing a body shell would be too expensive for them, they opted for a more basic single-seater racer; it became the successful Terrapin (pages 112-113). However, when Bob Coats and Murray Rose approached Staniforth in 1969 with plans for a Mini-based two-seater, it was a chance Staniforth had to take. Work started on the 'Whippingham Wrogue,' which used the Terrapin spaceframe chassis (drawing, right) as a base for the new two-seater. The Terrapin's original square tube chassis was developed into a significantly wider 60in base for the two-seater car, and was stress-panelled with sheet aluminium. The Terrapin's 84in wheelbase was retained, along with the location of the Mini engine just behind the seats. Mini subframes weren't used, but suspension parts like hubs and uprights were. The car used

specification

Car	**Sarcon Scarab**
Wheels driven	**Rear**
Built	**Yeadon (GB)**
Years	**1969-1972**
Number	**2**
Featured car	**Alastair Cox (GB)**

Drawings: Richard Blackmore

Scale in inches 0   6   12

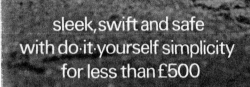

SCARAB

sleek, swift and safe
with do·it·yourself simplicity
for less than £500

SARCON LTD. SIZERS COURT · HENSHAW LANE · YEADON · LEEDS. TEL: RAWDON 4442.
MANUFACTURERS OF RACING CAR CHASSIS AND FIBREGLASS SPECIALISTS.

coil springs. A rather bulbous body was made from aluminium, and moulds were taken so fibreglass body shells could be made. The car used the Mini's original windscreen and headlights, while rear lights came from a Mini Van. Side and rear windows were Perspex, while the seats were moulded in fibreglass and trimmed in vinyl upholstery. Both the aluminium prototype body and the first fibreglass body were made into cars: one became a road car with detachable hardtop roof, the other an open sprint and hillclimb car. Staniforth tested them, achieving a top speed of 110mph and acceleration of 0-60 in 9 seconds.

The Whippingham Wrogue was ready to be marketed, and this is where Sarcon Limited of Yeadon, West Yorkshire came in. The company renamed it the Sarcon Scarab, had brochures made, and took it to a show in Birmingham. The car was offered for sale in 1971 as a kit. Any enthusiast could build it for less then £500, or so said the brochure: "You're not made of money! Neither is the Scarab." However, very quickly after the car's launch Sarcon Limited went into receivership in early 1972, although exactly what went wrong is a mystery. After only two prototypes, the Scarab was no more. The two cars were sold, and the fibreglass version was sprinted and hillclimbed regularly in the early seventies by Rick Branson. The aluminium prototype was sold in 2007, complete with the full set of original chassis jigs and body moulds.

Siva Buggy

After his MiniSprint adventure (pages 80-81), racer and designer Neville Trickett became involved with Siva Engineering in his native Dorset, surprising the world with some truly bizarre vehicles. In the late sixties and early seventies he launched an incredible number of new cars, of which some were stranger than fiction: Edwardian style 'horseless carriages' based on Fords, Volkswagens and 2CVs; the Ford-based Opus HRF; the Imp-based Siva Llama, and the incredibly futuristic looking Siva S160, Siva S350, Siva Saluki and

Siva V8. In-between designing and building these 'creatures,' Trickett found time to come up with a Mini-based buggy. It hadn't gone unnoticed to him that Volkswagen-based beach buggies were becoming a hit, and as a response to that Trickett decided to make one based on the Mini. For

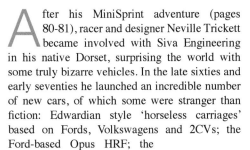

specification

Car	**Siva Buggy**
Wheels driven	**Front**
Built	**Bryanston/Poole (GB)/Amsterdam (NL)**
Years	**1970-1976**
Number	**94**
Featured car	**Rob Maas (NL)**

the price of £195 customers could buy a kit to build one themselves. The kit included a fibreglass body and a steel tube chassis frame that carried most of the Mini's suspension. Radius arms were lengthened, while the Mini's suspension trumpet cones were shortened. Headlights and rear lights were included, too. From a donor Mini the complete front subframe and engine could be bolted in, and other Mini parts – like instruments, pedals and wheels – could be re-used. Bucket seats, a black vinyl hood, and a flat, aluminium-framed windscreen were all extras, as were 13in wheels that gave the Buggy a better appearance than did the Mini's standard 10in wheels.

However, Trickett soon became fed up with his customers and decided to have the Siva Buggy distributed by motor accessory company Skyspeed in Feltham, which offered it as the Skyspeed-Siva Buggy. The company sold quite a few before the moulds and production rights were sold to Euromotor in Amsterdam, which had been importing Siva cars to Holland for a couple of years. Euromotor began building Trickett's design, and offered it for sale as the Siva Moonbug. By now, purple had become the standard colour for the car, with other colours available at extra cost. Production continued until 1976 when a fire destroyed the Amsterdam premises, along with the original moulds. In total, 94 cars are said to have been built.

Status 365

Brian Luff (pictured, opposite), an ex-Lotus Chief Engineer, had previously built the racy Status Minipower (page 104-105), but as that car proved very expensive to build Luff came up with a design for a totally different idea in 1974: the Status 365. It was based on Mini mechanicals, but this was about the only resemblance to Luff's earlier car. The 365 had to be cheaper and much more practical than the Minipower. The 365 name derived from the idea that it was meant to be useful all days of the year. Luff asked one of his fellow ex-Lotus mates, John Frayling, to design the car. It was Frayling who had been responsible for the lines of the Lotus Elite 'Type 75,' explaining the definite similarities with the 365. The fibreglass monocoque body shell of the 365 offered space for four people, and was of superior quality. The bodies offered for sale were all yellow, and Luff still remembers why: "If you mixed gel coat yourself you got a lot of bubbles in it, so we bought ready mixed, which you needed to buy in big quantities. We used marine gel coat, which was more flexible, and bought fifty-gallon drums. It was all yellow." Quite a lot of owners obviously liked their cars that way as many remained this colour.

specification

Car	**Status 365**
Wheels driven	**Front**
Built	**New Buckenham (GB)**
Years	**1974-1981**
Number	**Approximately 38**
Featured car	**Colin Carvel (GB)**

Luff doesn't have any official records on the number of cars built, but thinks there might have been 38: "It was all very informal and I also did some privately, you see." You could buy a body shell for £495 plus VAT and bolt on the Mini's front and rear subframes, including the engine, turning the car into a very modern Mini in 1974. The donor car's seats, instruments, and even floor coverings could be re-used as well.

Despite its durability not a lot of 365s appear to have survived. One of the very few still on the road is featured here. It is not an entirely standard example as the engine has been fitted to the rear of the car instead of the front. Although, perhaps this is not so strange; if you look closely at the artist's impression of the yellow car, drawn long before the first car was built, you see a Status 365 that is obviously rear-engined.

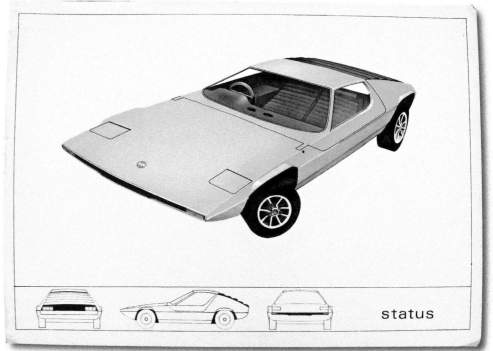

Status Minipower

Fed up with the numerous board meetings and bureaucratic paperwork at Lotus, Brian Luff gave up his job as Chief Engineer with the Norfolk-based sports car manufacturer in 1969. The Lotus Seven S4 had just been released and Luff didn't like it: "The size, the body, the pressed steel chassis – it was far from the original Seven concept," he recalls. Luff decided he could do better and set up the Status Motor Company. In its logo he envisaged the number 69 (the year he established the company), but also a yin-yang symbol and an eye. The name Status derived from the band Status Quo that Luff "quite liked". Three months after leaving Lotus his own tubular spaceframe chassis

was ready. It was a beautiful piece of engineering, with Formula 1-type suspension geometry that used double wishbones all round, combined with the Mini's front uprights and coil spring damper units. Any Mini engine could be connected to specially-machined driveshafts, thanks to the exceptionally wide track. According to the motoring press it was deemed 'the ultimate in clubman's road cars,' which was exactly how Luff had meant it to be. His original idea was to offer Lotus ride, roadholding and performance, coupled with Mini durability, running costs, parts availability and dealer service. The car was initially named Status Symbol, but later renamed Status Minipower to make it sound a

specification

Car	**Status Minipower**
Wheels driven	**Rear**
Built	**New Buckenham (GB)**
Years	**1971-1973**
Number	**20 chassis, 8 bodies**
Featured car	**Chris McMahon (GB)**

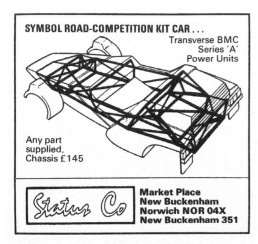

SYMBOL ROAD-COMPETITION KIT CAR...

Transverse BMC
Series 'A'
Power Units

Any part
supplied,
Chassis £145

Status Co

Market Place
New Buckenham
Norwich NOR 04X
New Buckenham 351

bit more serious. Customers could build it to their own specifications or follow the maker's ideas and use a complete set of parts offered by it. A chassis started at £490. Luff sold some chassis to motorsport enthusiasts, mainly autocrossers, who made up their own bodywork.

By 1971 Luff had finished a body pattern in his kitchen and fibreglass bodies of the Status Minipower were now offered. For £925 you had the complete set, less the engine. A hood or roof was not available, but by September 1972 Status did offer a fibreglass hardtop made to fit the Minipower. It seemed, however, that the car was over-engineered for its customers, who would have been happy with far less. Also, Luff found out too late that the cars were too costly: "All the bits were specific for the car: the gear change; the fuel tank; the pedals. It was far more expensive than a Lotus Seven to build." By late 1973 the 20th and final chassis was made. According to Luff only eight bodies were sold; survivors are rarely seen.

STATUS MK1 PRICE LIST

A. BASIC CHASSIS ASSEMBLY comprising:
Spaceframe: battery tray: all suspension parts to accept MINI uprights and brakes. Exchange
rear backplate: steering wheel, bedge, boss, column and clamps: pedal box assembly, throttle
cable, brake and clutch reservoir, master cylinders, pipes and fittings: handbrake cable and
stops: Fuel tank and straps: gear linkage: engine steady and standard exhaust.
£350.00

B. BASIC BODY ASSEMBLY comprising:
Self coloured body and bonnet: front wings with stays: headlamp pods with stays: rear wings
Black engine cover, hinges, clips and grille. Laminated windscreen, frame and pillars: Facia
blank: black cubby: filler cap assembly: Speedo cable: steel tail light panel: badge and letters.
£150.00

C. BASIC CHASSIS AND BODY ASSEMBLY
£500.00

Standard colours:- Italian Red, American White, French Blue, British Green, Belgium Yellow,
Status Tangerine, Status Black.

EXTRAS

1.	Carpets		£ 7.00 set
2.	Side trims		£ 7.00 pair
3.	Seat belts		£ 8.00 pair
4.	Seat base		£10.00
5.	Seat back		£10.00
6.	Head rests		£ 9.00 pair
7.	Hood and sticks		£28.00
8.	Side screens		£14.00 pair
9.	Roll over bar (bolt on)		£14.00
10.	De luxe Facia with switches and warning lights		£14.00
11.	De luxe Facia wiring harness		£20.00
12.	De luxe Facia Instruments at retail		£46.00
13.	Suspension units adjustable for damping and ride level complete with special springs. (strongly recommended)		£13.00 pair
14.	Mamba, McNally or Revolution 6" x 10" wheels with Goodyear Rally tyres at retail price, around		£80.00 set of 4
15.	Mini heater mounting brackets		£ 3.00 set
16.	Engine steadies		£ 5.00 pair
17.	3 branch exhaust system		£20.00
18.	Pedal box adjusters		£ 1.00
19.	Aluminium tail light panel		£ 4.00
20.	Rectangular headlamp pods to suit Lucas (Avenger) lens		£ 6.00 pair
21.	Rear wing air ducts		£ 6.00 pair
D.	Chassis body kit with extras 1-19		£896.00
E.	Chassis body kit with extras 1-19 and new, reconditioned or sound BLMH parts, and new tail lights, excluding power plant.		£939.00
F.	As E but with Status specification Osselli 1275 engine with BMC reconditioned gearbox		£1184.00

TERMS

EITHER   30% deposit with order and balance prior to delivery.

OR   5% discount for payment with order

DELIVERY METHOD

EITHER   Customer to collect from Norwich

OR   Delivery at 12½p per mile

DELIVERY TIME

Approximately 8 weeks from receipt of order.

Stimson Mini Bug Mk1/Mk2

In 1968, whilst in Canada designing wooden houses, Barry Stimson (pictured) came across a Myers Manx beach buggy, immediately liking it: "I thought it was so refreshingly different, so I decided to design one myself. Not Volkswagen-based but around the Mini." On the plane back to England Stimson made an initial sketch (right), and began work on a prototype back home in Chichester. He rented a hangar in Brighton, starting on a tiny budget. Stimson: "Anything that vaguely had the shape you needed was used. The headlamp pods were moulded from a bra." When the first Stimson Mini Bug was finished in early 1970 the result looked surprisingly like his early sketch. Reactions were quite overwhelming and the little Mini-based buggy even appeared

on national television in the *It's Cliff Richard* show. Under the car's doorless and roofless fibreglass body could be found a simple square tube frame, to which the Mini's front subframe was mounted. The rear used the Mini's trailing arms and motorcycle coils springs and damper units, while the floor was plywood. It was sold as a basic kit minus the engine for £170, and a complete car was offered from £295. Initially, the car had

specification

Car	**Stimson Mini Bug Mk1/Mk2**
Wheels driven	**Front**
Built	**Chichester (GB)**
Years	**1970-1971/1971-1973**
Number	**Approximately 20/approximately 160**
Featured car	**Ivo Krul (NL)**

the optional extra of a low Perspex windscreen, but when this was found to be illegal a more conventional glass screen was offered.

By the end of 1970 Stimson had sold around twenty Mini Bugs in total. A slightly redesigned Mk2 arrived early in 1971, and interest increased. As a matter-of-fact British Leyland was interested, too, and went to examine the car. Barry Stimson: "They wanted to know all about the stress tests we had put it through. I said we had a fat friend and we got him to bounce up and down on the chassis. If it bent we welded another strut in. We never heard a thing of them anymore." Stimson

also persuaded Jacky Stewart to drive a Mini Bug on the F1 course in Monaco. Stimson's business partner, Ian Smith, drove the car down to France, but *Telegraph* journalist David Benson crashed it just before Stewart was to take it over for the parade preceding the race.

Some Mini Bugs were used on race and grass tracks, and a racing version named CS+I with a triangular spaceframe was offered in 1972, but only four were sold. From 1976 to 1986 various companies tried to revive the Mini Bug, but it was never the success it had been in the early seventies.

Stimson Safari Six

Barry Stimson's company, formed in 1969 to build Mini Bugs, was renamed several times during its first few years of business. By 1972 it was under the name Design Developments, at which point Stimson found it time for a second car, the Stimson Safari Six; a twelve-foot-long six-wheeled pick-up also based on Mini mechanicals. It was meant as a practical vehicle designed to carry out a multitude of jobs, as well as being just a little extraordinary for folks who liked to be noticed. According to Stimson it was a bit of a mix between the Mini Pick-up, Moke and Traveller, but also a Range Rover and Renault 4. It was offered for sale in 1972 at £800 all in, which meant it was even delivered with a hood that covered not just the driver and passenger, but also the complete rear of the car. It also had

a zip-up side screen that could be used as a door for the driver. Stimson used the Mini's standard windscreen for the Safari Six, but placed it within a new frame, to which the weather equipment could be attached with push buttons. Power came from a reconditioned Mini 850 unit. Like the Mini Bug, the Safari Six was based on a tubular chassis to which a Mini engine subframe and fibreglass

specification

Car	**Stimson Safari Six**
Wheels driven	**Front**
Built	**Westbourne (GB)**
Years	**1972-1973**
Number	**Approximately 20**
Featured car	**Cora & Bill Oldham (GB)**

body was attached. Body panels were colour impregnated in Pirate Red or Golden Yellow, and were easy to replace. The rear four wheels used Mini swinging arms with Girling spring/damper units. With twelve extra inches the rear track was considerably wider than that of a Mini, helping the designer to create a large pick-up rear deck, complete with fold down bench seat and lockable under-floor 'boot.'

Stimson was asked to take the Safari Six over to Malta to display it at an exhibition of British design in 1974. It was the star of the show, but by then production had finished. The Safari Six had been a rather big investment for Design Developments and after only a year the company went into receivership. Approximately twenty Safari Sixes were built.

The rights of the car were taken over by the Welsh company Automotive Services, which planned to relaunch the vehicle as the Shikari with a Ford Fiesta or Peugeot engine, but it never happened. Barry Stimson went on to design more unusual vehicles, of which the Stimson Scorcher and Stimson Trek (page 123) were just two.

Taylorspeed Mini Jem

L ike the Broadspeed GT, the Mini Jem was made under licence in Australia. This time it was racer, tuner and car dealer John Taylor who was granted licence to fabricate and sell the car. Taylor ran a Lotus and Aston Martin dealership in Adelaide, but also offered Mini tuning kits under the Taylorspeed name. It was in 1968 that he signed an agreement with Fellpoint Limited, who built the Mini Jem in Penn, Buckinghamshire. Fellpoint had begun working on the Mini Jem Mk2, but the body shell that was sent over to Australia, from which to fabricate a mould, was naturally a Mk1. The job of creating the mould was carried out at a surfboard factory in Adelaide (above, right).

specification

Car	**Taylorspeed Mini Jem**
Wheels driven	**Front**
Built	**Adelaide (AUS)**
Years	**1968-1972**
Number	**10**
Featured car	**Syd Crawford (AUS)**

The Taylorspeed Mini Jem was introduced at the Royal Adelaide Exhibition in September 1968, although it did not differ much from the English Jems. Later versions, however, had more features common with Australian-built Minis. The interior sported different fascia and instruments, the door handles had changed, and the Perspex rear screen now had a square bottom. The car was offered for sale as a kit in four variants:

110

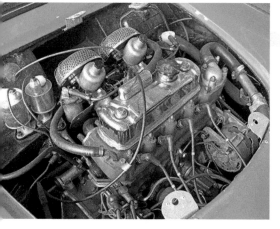

'Kit A' came as a prime painted and untrimmed shell with doors, bonnet and untrimmed bucket seats at AU $890; the later 'Kit D' came as a complete car without engine at AU $1690. There was a long list of extras, ranging from an electric fan to a close ratio gearbox. According to Taylorspeed a car enthusiast would be able to build a Mini Jem in approximately 50 hours. *Sports Car World* magazine test drove a Cooper S-powered Mini Jem, clocking 0-50 mph in 5.5 seconds. According to John Taylor that particular car "had seen 120mph on a cool evening." Taylor showed correspondent Barry Cartford how to drive it. Cartford wrote: "Under constant power the car could be set up in an understeer attitude, but lift off and the tail immediately shoots out in oversteer – plant the foot and we head for the inside of the curve. A bit dicey for the average enthusiast – and me!"

Despite all its efforts Taylorspeed made no more than 10 bodies, although some of these came to life unofficially when the moulds were found in the Adelaide surf shop years later. Seven cars are believed to still exist.

Terrapin

The Terrapin is the only Mini derivative that has had its own book, *High Speed, Low Cost*. Its author, Allan Staniforth, was so enthusiastic about the Mini-engined Terrapin he had designed and built he decided to share his experiences with the world. First published in 1969, the book offered buyers a set of full-scale drawings for an extra £4.50 by filling in the tear-out coupon and sending it to the author.

Staniforth was a reporter for the *Daily Mirror*, and he liked a bit of motorsport in his spare time. He was one of the very first to race a Mini in early 1960, becoming quite successful in hillclimbs. When Staniforth met Richard Blackmore in 1964 the two men began working on ideas for building their own Mini-based car. At first they considered a two-seater, but they soon dropped the idea, designing a single-seater for sprinting and hillclimbing. They came up with the name Terrapin as it rhymed with 'Min,' but also, as Staniforth explains: "it was one of the few animals, fish or birds that hadn't been nobbled by someone else already as the name for a car!" Staniforth and Blackmore made a 1:8 scale model in balsa

specification

Car	**Terrapin**
Wheels driven	**Rear**
Built	**Horsforth (GB)**
Years	**1965-on**
Number	**Approximately 80**
Featured car	**Robert MacKnay (GB)**

supercharger. He even took a few international speed records.

Staniforth's book, republished in 2003, became a standard for sprinting and hillclimbing enthusiasts wishing to build their own cars. Terrapins are still being built to this day, the car featured here being one of them.

wood and soon started working on a chassis. It was made of square tubes with pop-riveted sheet aluminium sides, and designed to have the Mini engine at the rear, which was initially fitted with a bored-out 997cc Cooper. The suspension used four Mini front uprights and hubs, while widened Mini 10in wheels were used at the front and Vauxhall Viva 12in wheels at the rear. The nose came from a 1959 Cooper Formula 2 car, and was narrowed and lowered.

The first Terrapin was completed only four hours before it was due to be in the paddock for its first outing at the Harewood hillclimb. Staniforth entered the car in numerous events, winning quite a few. He was clocked at over 140mph, having fitted 13in rear wheels and a 1060cc engine with Arnott

TiCi

With a length of only 89 inches the TiCi (pronounced 'titchy') was said to be the shortest road car ever when it was introduced in late 1971. The car was the project of Anthony Hill, who was a furniture lecturer at the Loughborough College of Art and Design. Two years earlier Hill had made a similar, but even smaller, city car that was powered by a 500cc Triumph motorcycle engine, but that remained a one-off. The two-seater TiCi seemed a more serious car, and when ERA-founder Raymond Mays decided to support the project there seemed to be nothing in its way.

The car's fibreglass body shell came in four pieces: front, engine-cover, dashboard and the actual monocoque. The latter piece even included moulded-in seats. The use of colour-coded gell coat meant the car colour was always bright yellow. A Mini front subframe, with engine and all suspension parts, but locked steering, was bolted in at the rear of the car, just behind the seats. The

front suspension used Mini links and coil spring/damper units. A specially-made six-gallon steel fuel tank was fitted centrally in the interest of safety.

As well as being exhibited at the motor shows of London and Barcelona, Stirling Moss

specification

Car	**TiCi**
Wheels driven	**Rear**
Built	**Sutton-in-Ashfield (GB)**
Years	**1972-1973**
Number	**40**
Featured car	**Ian Mitcheson (GB)**

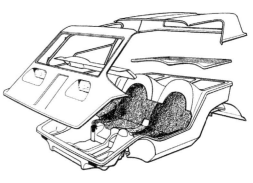

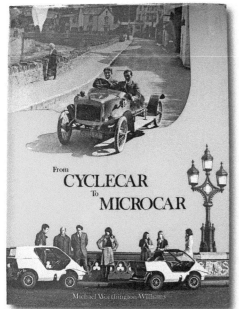

helped promote the TiCi by driving it in busy London traffic with 'dolly birds' in the car. In early 1972 the car was offered for sale as a complete kit with step-by-step instructions for £395. A hardtop and doors were available as an extra for £35. "There is no need for improvisation or of specialist knowledge to build a TiCi," mentioned the brochure. "If you're capable of removing Mini parts properly then you should be able to construct your own TiCi in a couple of weekends."

Despite the promotional efforts and the financial backing of Raymond Mays, who thought it could become a big seller, the TiCi wasn't much of a success. A year after its introduction only 40 kits were sold, and by that time VAT rules for kit cars made it much too expensive. One of the 40 cars went to British entrepreneur Clive Sinclair, who converted his TiCi to electric power.

Unipower GT Mk1

Often considered the best Mini-based car, the Unipower GT was born when Rootes engineer and Elva racing team manager Ernie Unger met freelance designer Val Dare-Bryan at Goodwood in 1963. The two men decided to build their own Mini-powered GT car, and started working on a test mule in Dare-Bryans workshop in Surrey. It had a spaceframe and independent wheel suspension all round that used Mini uprights, modified Mini suspension arms and coils springs front and rear. An old 850cc Mini Van engine was swung through 180 degrees and placed just behind the driver.

Tony Lanfranchi tested the car without the body shell at Brands Hatch, calling it 'the flying bedstead; he couldn't find much wrong with it. Meanwhile, a body for the car was designed by a Ford stylist, who wished to remain anonymous after drawing the car while his bosses thought he was working on the GT40. A windscreen and its steel frame were sourced from a Triumph GT6,

while other parts came from Ford, Austin, Jensen and Vauxhall. A second spaceframe was finished and delivered to Robert Peel & Company in Kingston-upon-Thames, where an aluminium body was made (pictured, right). Specialised Mouldings Limited was sub-contracted to replicate fibreglass bodies from it, and Arch Motors were to weld the spaceframes.

It was now 1965, and Unger and Dare-Bryan were running out of money. They needed some financial support to put their car – christened Hustler GT – into production; they found a backer in Tim Powell. Powell was a powerboat racing champion whose company, Universal Power Drives, manufactured forklift trucks and mechanical winches, and could do with an image boost.

specification

Car	**Unipower GT Mk1**
Wheels driven	**Rear**
Built	**Perivale (GB)**
Years	**1966-1968**
Number	**60**
Featured car	**Mark Butler (GB)**

A corner of his factory in Middlesex was set aside, and the name of the car changed to Unipower GT. It was launched at the 1966 Racing Car Show where it was very well received. Universal Power Drives offered the car for sale at £950 with a 998cc Cooper engine, while a 1275cc Cooper S-engined Unipower came in at £1150. However, development hadn't completely finished, so it wasn't until late 1966 that the first car left the factory. The gear-linkage, operated from the sill at the driver's side, took time to sort out, and the radiator was repositioned to the nose

of the car. The Unipower GT returned to the Racing Car Show in 1967, creating plenty of interest once again, but by November 1968 only sixty cars had been sold and Powell lost interest. A planned targa version was cancelled.

Unipower GT Mk2

The development of the Unipower GT Mk1 had not been easy and Tim Powell of Universal Power Drives became fed up with the project by the end of 1968. Having sold only sixty cars it seemed impossible to speed up production significantly. Powell decided to sell the company, finding interest in 22-year-old racing driver Piers Weld-Forrester. Weld-Forester moved production to a very well-equipped plant in London, naming his new motoring concern UWF, for 'Unger Weld-Forrester.' Once again the Racing Car Show became the showground for the revised Unipower GT, which was exhibited in 1969.

The Mk2 came with an interior that provided much more comfort, with repositioned instruments, black padded fascia, and softer springs in the

suspension. The rear lights, which had previously come from a Vauxhall Viva, were now replaced with bigger clusters. The gear stick mounted in the sill of the driver's door remained, but a five-speed Jack Knight gearbox was now available, too.

Various distributors throughout the UK were appointed, and the future looked bright for the Mk2. However, trouble started when Weld-Forrester began to concentrate on a comprehensive racing

specification

Car	**Unipower GT Mk2**
Wheels driven	**Rear**
Built	**London (GB)**
Years	**1968-1969**
Number	**15**
Featured cars	**Gerry Hulford (GB); Turtle Trading Ltd (J)**

Unipower GT Mk2

publicity campaign. He had three lightweight works cars built and entered one in the Targa Florio in June 1969. It was air-freighted to Sicily where the car came twelfth in practice, but was crashed by a mechanic on the night preceding the race. Another racer was built to compete in the Le Mans 24-hour Race in July of that year. That car, shown here in yellow, was entered privately by Weld-Forester, and featured a Janspeed 1340cc Cooper S engine. During practice it was reputedly clocked at 140mph on the Mulsanne Straight, the French nicknaming it 'la puce jaune' (the yellow flea). It later lost a wheel at high speed, although there was no serious damage, but when the engine blew up after three hours practice it could no longer be raced. There were similar troubles in the Gran Premio Mugello, the Grand Prix of Denmark and the 12-hour race of Barcelona, all during the 1969 season.

Meanwhile, in London, the workforce were simply unable to finish the required five cars a month that Weld-Forester and Unger had planned for, and together with the extraordinary high costs of racing, the company closed in December 1969. Only fifteen Mk2s had been built. Eight years later, in October 1977, Piers Weld-Forester was killed in a motorcycle crash during a race at Brands Hatch.

Zagato Mini Gatto

The year 1961 was a remarkable one for Zagato. The Milanese coachbuilders had just launched the Aston Martin DB4 GT Zagato and were working on the Alfa-Romeo Giulietta SZ Coda Tronca. They also had another project of a very different kind: the Zagato Mini Gatto, built on the base of a brand new 1961 Morris Mini Van. Like the Aston and Alfa the design came from Ercole Spada, (pictured) who worked for Zagato. Spada also chose the name Gatto – Italian for cat – as the car's headlights reminded him of a cat.

The Zagato Mini Gatto was built for Vicenze Piatti, who had successfully built and marketed the Piatti scooters during the fifties, and later patented the twin-spin combustion chamber. The Mini Van's floorpan was retained on the Gatto, and an aluminium body attached to the underpinnings with thin steel strips. The luxurious interior came in maroon velvet, featuring a comfortable rear seat 'hung' in the rear of the car. Some parts, such as the aluminium door handles, were sourced from other Zagato models, but Spada and the Zagato team used anything they could get their hands on, which accounted for the set of Lancia keys that came with the car. Under the bonnet a tuned 998cc Cooper engine came fitted with specially-developed Dellorto carburettors.

The car was test-driven by several British motoring journalists who were all surprised by its nippy character and low fuel economy. The 'Mini-Zagato', as it was called, was shown at the

specification

Car	**Zagato Mini Gatto**
Wheels driven	**Front**
Built	**Milan (I)**
Years	**1961**
Number	**1**
Featured car	**Mingori family (I)**

Earls Court Motor Show in 1961 where a price tag of £1200 was mentioned – more than twice the price of the donor Mini Van. The idea was to set up a production line in the UK and produce the car in limited numbers, although it soon turned out the British Motor Corporation was not particularly happy with the idea. BMC's Lord Stokes claimed it conflicted with his Mini programme, and he did not want to collaborate by supplying cars or parts; this ultimately killed the Gatto. Zagato tried again a year later, applying similar aluminium clothing to a Hillman Imp, but only three 'Zimps' were sold. Piatti drove his unique Mini in Milan for a few more years before parking it in a shed where it has stood ever since.

The cars that didn't make it

As mentioned in the introduction, not all the Mini derivatives are featured in this book. Some of them would have been rather obvious; there is no Alto Duo, no Freestyle, no Hustler and no GTM Rossa, for example. In other cases it proved too difficult to find enough information to describe them over a two-page spread. This chapter is to compensate for that shortcoming.

It is the obscure cars that haunt me most. Not so much the one-offs built by enthusiasts, like the Micron GT (1) of brothers Brian and Rex Bray, or the Davenport Special (2) by Derek Davenport, but cars such as the Lawther GT (3). This one-off just seemed very professional, built back in 1967 by draughtsman Robert Lawther, who later became a helicopter designer. I came across some lovely old pictures of the car and was very close to its current home, but unfortunately, was unable to photograph it and therefore left it out.

There was the eccentric Saga (4), built in 1966 by former Elva employee Brian Diss. The car was owned for decades by a Sussex driving school teacher, who couldn't remember to whom he sold it. What a pity.

For the Killeen K16 (5) of the early seventies I couldn't find any good connection to start a search, while the Timeire (6), built and raced by Irishman Tim Conroy (hence the name), seemed no longer to exist.

The Canadian Reptune GT (7) proved difficult, too, as none of the supposed four cars built were apparently

DIY BUDGET POWER!

HOT CAR POWER & CUSTOM

DEC. 1975 ● 30p

10 SETS OF PIRELLI TYRES TO BE WON!

JOH 235N

● Home built Mini special
● Project street rod-new series ▶
● Handling hop-up ● BMC diff swops
● Transplant special–Cortina V8

ANR 608B

The cars that didn't make it

9

in driveable condition. There have been a few rip-offs of the Stimson Mini Bug that I couldn't find more information about, such as: the Cirrus and the Luna Bug (8), of which the latter is a true, and shameless, Stimson copy. Speaking of Stimson, I did photograph a rare Stimson Trek (9), as well as a Stimson Scorcher (10), and was provided with plenty of information by Barry Stimson himself. However, as the crazy Scorcher only had three wheels it didn't make it to a two page spread, and there simply was no place left for the Trek. Sorry Barry!

5

6

7

8

10

The cars that didn't make it

Like Stimson, Brian Luff was involved in quite a few Mini-based vehicles, too. Unfortunately, I couldn't track down the Sabot (11) prototype he sold a couple of years ago. The Phoenix (12) that both Luff and ex-Lotus man Paul Hausauer were

involved with would not have been any easier, but there were still many other interesting cars. The Seagull (13), from Aldershot, Hants, was just not interesting enough, so I didn't even start a search.

A car that did trigger my imagination was 'Project X' (14), built by some of the editorial staff at *Australian Sports Car World* magazine in 1964 and 1965. The building process was covered throughout the magazine and it made the cover in July 1965. Craig Watson, who helped me in tracking down the Australian Mini derivatives, believes the car still exists, but was unable to find it in time for inclusion.

Another one-off that intrigued me was the Mini Jem Estate (15), an early Mk2 built by Fellpoint Limited. However,

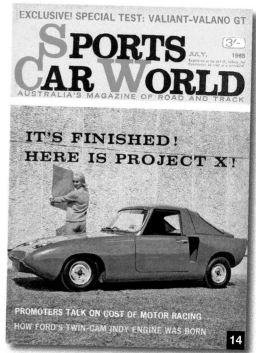

15

16

17

18

19

apart from some grimy pictures I couldn't find any information at all. The same went for the ultra-low Aurora BMC (16), as well as the Belgian Méan Sonora (17), although I did find a cool brochure. Are there any examples left out there?

Just before this book went into print fellow motoring journalist Chris Rees sent me a picture of a pretty Mini-based hatchback, not knowing what it was. It turned out to be the Codford Mini (18), built in the Wiltshire village of the same name by MiniSprint and Siva Buggy instigator Neville Trickett. Supposedly, Trickett designed the car in 1966 and at least two were built that year. However, I wasn't able to track down any survivors.

Another car with an even smarter background was the IGM Minbug (19), designed and built by Formula 1 ace Gordon Murray just before getting his job at Brabham's in 1970! Murray believes the Minbug helped him get the Brabham post by turning up for his interview in the car: "The co-owner of the company, Ron Tauranac, who interviewed me was a very practical sort of engineer and that sort of thing would have been far more impressive to him than an engineering degree." Murray built

four Minbugs in total, all of them were thought lost until I came across one during the completion of this book! I bought it sight unseen and Murray is now planning to restore it.

There must be other Mini derivatives of which I know nothing. If I missed other deserving cars, or if you have more information about the cars featured in this book, I invite you to get in touch with me via Veloce Publishing. Perhaps the missing cars you tell me about will make it to a second volume of *Maximum Mini*.

Bibliography

Picture resources

All pictures of the featured cars have been photographed by the author, except: Broadspeed GT (by Brian Foley), Buckle Monaco, Bulanti, De Joux Mini GT, Ecurie de Dez, Lolita Mk1, Lolita Mk2, Nota Fang and Taylorspeed Mini Jem, photographed by Craig Watson; the green Fletcher GT photographed by Kiain Balloch; the Landar R7 photographed by Carl Braun; the Pellandini photographed by Max Kinsmore; the Sarcon Scarab photographed by Alistair Cox, and the Status Minipower photographed by the LAT archive.

All additional pictures are from the author's personal archive, complemented by images sourced from Autopics, Ferrett Photography, LAT archive, and numerous private collections. Noteworthy for their contributions are Bob Blackman, Richard Butterfield, Carl Braun, Tony 'Podge' Dealey, Naoki Ishizuka, Brian Luff, Kazuo Maruyama, Bill Needham, Paul Pellandine, Hans-Peter Seufert, Barry Stimson, Paolo di Taranto and Andrea Zagato.

Books

Amazing Mini, Peter Filby, Gentry Books, 1981
British Specialist Cars, Chris Rees, Windrow & Greene, 1993
British Specialist Cars, Volume 1, Jasper Wilkins, Bookstop, 1977
British Specialist Cars, Volume 2, Peter Filby, Bookstop, 1977
Classic Kit Cars, Chris Rees, Bluestream Books, 1997
Great Australian Sports Cars & Specials, Mike McCarthy, Wildcat Press, 1987
High Speed, Low Cost, Allan Staniforth, Blackfriars Press, 1969
Mini – the Racing Story, John Baggott, The Crowood Press, 1999
Morgan Maverick, Christopher Lawrence, Douglas Loveridge Publications, 2008
Specialist Sports Cars, Peter Filby, David & Charles, 1974
Specialist Sports Cars, Richard Hesseltine, Haynes Publishing, 2001

Magazines

Auto Italiana
Cars & Car Conversions
Component Car
Custom Car
Hot Car
Kit Car
Kitcars International
Mini Magazine
MiniWorld
Sports Car World
Small Car
The Mini Experience
Which Kit?

Index